2.95
1.95

JESUS
the
Powerful
SERVANT

LIFE OF CHRIST GROWTH GUIDE

by Clark Peddicord
Illustrated by Peter Pohle

Campus Crusade for Christ International
Published by
HERE'S LIFE PUBLISHERS, INC.
San Bernardino, California 92402

LIFE OF CHRIST GROWTH GUIDE
BOOK 1: JESUS, THE POWERFUL SERVANT
by Clark Peddicord
Illustrated by Peter Pohle
(Peter Pohle is a graduate of the College of Fine Arts in Berlin
and works as a graphic artist with the Campus Crusade for
Christ team in West Germany.)

A Campus Crusade for Christ book
Published by
HERE'S LIFE PUBLISHERS, INC.
P.O. Box 1576
San Bernardino, California 92402

Library of Congress Catalogue Card 83-073129
ISBN 0-86605-119-8
HLP Product No. 403329
©1984, Here's Life Publishers, Inc.

Printed in the United States of America.

Scripture quotations are from the New American Standard Bible,
© The Lockman Foundation 1960, 1962, 1963, 1968, 1971, 1972,
1973, 1975, and are used by persmission.

FOR MORE INFORMATION, WRITE:

L.I.F.E.—P.O. Box A399, Sydney South 2000, Australia
Campus Crusade for Christ of Canada—Box 368, Abbottsford, B.C., V25 4N9, Canada
Campus Crusade for Christ—103 Friar Street, Reading RGI IEP, Berkshire, England
Lay Institute for Evangelism—P.O. Box 8786, Auckland 3, New Zealand
Great Commission Movement of Nigeria—P.O. Box 500, Jos, Plateau State Nigeria,
West Africa
Life Ministry—P.O. Box/Bus 91015, Auckland Park 2006, Republic of So. Africa
Campus Crusade for Christ Int'l.—Arrowhead Springs, San Bernardino, CA 92414,
U.S.A.

CONTENTS

INTRODUCTION

WHO IS THIS STUDY FOR?

This *Life of Christ Growth Guide, Book 1: Jesus, the Powerful Servant,* is designed as a personal or group workbook for those who want to discover Jesus for themselves.

Jesus is the center of the Christian faith. Yet, many of us who call ourselves Christians have only a blurred picture of His life. We have wrapped His story in tinsel and glitter. The real Jesus is hardly known among us—the Jesus who was most at home among the hungry, homeless, lonely and oppressed. This workbook will help remedy this.

Jesus, the Powerful Servant, will help you:

Discover for yourself the person of Christ through investigating the major events of His life recorded in the Gospels.

Develop a clear picture of how Jesus related to God and to other people—His personal character and what it was like to live with and be around Him.

Discover what following Christ—"discipleship"— means. Guided application questions will help you transfer the truth you learn to your daily life.

Greatly expand your knowledge of the cultural background of the Bible and improve your skill in understanding its message.

Learn the principles of good interpretation and be better equipped to interpret the Bible for yourself.

SUGGESTIONS FOR GROUP BIBLE STUDY LEADERS

When this *Life of Christ Growth Guide, Book 1: Jesus, the Powerful Servant*, is used for group Bible study, group members will learn together what following Christ means. They will learn valuable Bible study skills and communication skills as they share their insights, questions and personal discoveries with one another.

1. *Organize Your Group Carefully*

Ask God to lead you to several others who want to discover more about following Jesus through group Bible study. These may include friends at work or church, neighbors, or fellow students. Tell them specifically why you want to start a Bible study group. Stress that the meetings will be friendly and open times of sharing and mutual encouragement. Be sure to tell them the place and time of the study. Assure each person that the spiritual benefits gained through this kind of Bible study are outstanding.

Generally, it takes six to ten persons to have an effective group. Each session should be held in an informal setting: a comfortable living room, a private room in a restaurant, or a dormitory room. Someone may serve light refreshments at either the beginning or close of the study session.

A good seating arrangement is crucial. Ideally, each group member should be able to see everyone in the group. So, if possible, arrange chairs in a circle or semi-circle.

2. *Build an Open and Supportive Atmosphere*

Spend a few minutes at the beginning of each session to get better acquainted with each other. Encourage everyone to talk about their victories and concerns. Ask two or three to pray about these things. Ask them to praise God for their victories and request His specific help in facing the challenges and concerns that were shared.

Assure the group that no comment or question raised during a session will be ridiculed or ignored. Each participant should feel secure about entering into the discussion and know he or she is a cherished and respected member of the circle. Thank everyone for participating and compliment the group on their openness and their learning. If you find that someone has a tendency to dominate discussions, you may find it helpful to make the rule: "No one may answer more than two questions consecutively."

3. *Serve as a Discussion Leader*

Your role in group Bible study is that of a discussion leader. A wise discussion leader does not lecture throughout a session. Instead, the leader should relate to the group like a coach does to a team. Just as a coach helps develop the skills of the players and motivates them to do their best, so a discussion leader shows the participants how to study the Bible and apply it to daily living. He motivates them to dig into the Scriptures diligently and enthusiastically.

These studies are based upon the students' doing the assignments before they come to the group Bible study session. A scheduled time and an active pen or pencil are basic to effective personal Bible study. Encourage the members of your group to set aside a regular study time and guard it well. Convince them of their need for Bible study. Jerome, the famous translator of the Bible into Latin, said, "Ignorance of the Bible is ignorance of Christ." During their personal preparation time they should keep their pen or pencil busy recording their thoughts and reactions to what they are discovering. An inch of ink is worth a mile of memory.

4. *Lead Your Group Through Each Section of the Study*

You can use the five sections of each lesson as "road signs" to guide the group through the study session.

 Introduction—As the leader, you should summarize this section in your own words or read it aloud to the group. It will set the stage for your discussion.

 Life Principle—Ask someone to read this section aloud from the Growth Guide. You can introduce it by saying,

"The *Life Principle* spells out the purpose of this lesson. John (or Mary), why don't you read it out loud so we can have it fresh in our minds?"

You could then ask someone else:

"Mike, can you help us put that into our own words? What do you see as the main point of this lesson for us?"

 Investigation—This is the meat of each lesson. Each one in the study group will have made new and personal discoveries about Christ and the life of discipleship during the time of personal preparation. Your goal as a study leader is to draw out and summarize these discoveries. You can do this by using the *starred questions*. In each lesson there are three or four questions with a star (*) beside them. These questions are especially good for group discussion times.

Draw out the group in *three steps:*

Step One: Focus on a question.

Suggest to the group: "Why don't we take a look at question number _____ (one of the starred questions)? Susan, would you read it for us?" (Susan reads the question aloud.)

Step Two: Expand the discussion.

Ask a member of the group, "Alice, what do you think about this?" In this way you can lead the group into a discussion of the question. Let volunteers share their answers and tell why they answered as they did. Always be alert to ask "What do you think this could mean for us? What implications does it have for our lives?"

Step Three: Summarize the discussion.

When you have the impression that the group should move on, you should *summarize:* "What I think we've seen from this question is..." (Then mention two or three insights shared by the participants. A good Bible study leader will keep in mind one or two points made by the others during the discussion so they can be used in this way.)

Then say, "Are there any other insights that could help us? If not, let's move on to question _____" (the next starred question).

At this point you begin the discussion process again:

"John, why don't you read it aloud for us?" *Never* ridicule anyone's answer or opinion. If you think someone's answer is wrong or not clear, simply redirect the discussion to the group: "That's a thought. How do the rest of you feel about that?" Usually the group will bring things into a proper balance, and you can move on to the next point.

Let the group members raise their own questions, based on the passage. And, whenever possible, let the answers to these questions also come from the group.

Application—Here the mind and heart team up to face together the issues, needs and concerns of daily life. Again, as in the previous section, you can lead the group in three steps:

Step One: Focus on a question.

Suggest to the study circle, "Let's move on and reflect a little on how this all applies to our daily lives. Let's look at the 'Application' section together." At this point you may want to read aloud the short paragraph that introduces the questions in this section.

Step Two: Expand the discussion.

Then, ask, "How did we answer these questions—how can we apply this study to our lives? What do you think?" If there is hesitation, you can pick out one of the more confident participants and say, "Mary, will you help us get started? How do you feel about this?"

Step Three: Summarize the discussion.

When you feel the group should move on, *summarize* the discussion: "I guess what we're saying about applying this to our lives is . . . (mention two or three insights shared)."

If you feel the study session is at a high point after discussing the "Application" section, you can suggest closing the study with prayer, and omit the last section:

"Let's talk to God in prayer about these things."

You may want to have the group set a few spiritual goals, then ask for a progress report in later study sessions.

 Principles of Good Interpretation—Occasionally, if you think the group would be helped by a discussion of this section, suggest:

"Let's take a look finally at the last section of the study. Did anyone gain some new insights into how to better understand and interpret the Bible?" Allow a moment for the group to review the section. Then you can close the time with prayer as suggested under the last section.

5. *Conclude Your Session on a Positive Note*

Briefly summarize the progress of the group—what was learned and how the group plans to apply the truths gained from the study. This will give everyone a sense of accomplishment as well as a sense of accountability to put what they have studied into practice.

Before you end the study session, tell the participants what the next study will cover and encourage them to begin their personal preparation early in the week. Don't forget to remind them about the time and location of the next group meeting!

6. *Keep Within a Realistic Time Frame*

How much time your group devotes to each section of a lesson depends upon the intensity and depth of the discussion. The following time frame is a good guideline. Be flexible in altering the time slots to fit the needs and preferences of your group.

1.	Open the study session sharing, short prayer	15 minutes
2.	Discuss the sections of the Growth Guide:	
	Introduction and Key Principle	15 minutes
	Interpretation	30 minutes
	Application and Principles of Good Interpretation	15-30 minutes
3.	Conclude the session—prayer, remind the group of next meeting	5 minutes
	TOTAL	90 minutes

Additional Study Resources:

You, as the group leader, may want to use some additional study resources to prepare for the study. This is not necessary since the studies are filled with a wealth of background material. However, if you feel inclined to dig further, two of the best single-volume books available on the life of Christ are:

Everett F. Harrison, *A Short Life of Christ.* Grand Rapids: Eerdmans, 1968.

Donald Guthrie, *Jesus the Messiah.* Grand Rapids: Eerdmans, 1972.

Since the Gospel of Mark is often the central text in the studies, you may find one or both of the following commentaries helpful:

William Lane, *Commentary on the Gospel of Mark.* Grand Rapids: Eerdmans, 1974.

C.E.B. Cranfield, *The Gospel According to St. Mark.* Cambridge: Cambridge University Press, 1977.

STUDY 1
THE BACKGROUND
TO CHRIST'S COMING

 INTRODUCTION

Jesus entered the stage of history at precisely the right time. The world had been carefully prepared. The apostle Paul describes it as "the fullness of time" or "when the time had fully come," and in this first study you will discover just how God had prepared the world for Jesus' arrival. Jesus did not come to a pretty, happy world. He came to a world of violence, greed, and oppression—a world like ours. He did not come as a member of the ruling race or class. Though He had all the power and authority of heaven available to Him, He came as a simple servant.

LIFE PRINCIPLE: How to see God's infinite concern for the world.

God's careful preparation of the world for Christ's coming demonstrates His infinite concern that all men and women understand the message of the gospel.

In this lesson you will study how the world was prepared for Christ's coming:

— You will examine God's original purpose for us, how mankind turned away from God's plan, and how God's ancient promises pointed the way toward Jesus.

— You will investigate the Jewish, Greek and Roman cultural background of the time of Jesus and learn how each culture helped to prepare the world for His coming.

— You will study some of the reasons the Gospels were written.

INVESTIGATION

The Spiritual Background to Christ's Coming

To understand the story of Jesus one has to begin at the very beginning of everything and study God's original purpose for the human race.

The first chapter of the book of Genesis clearly explains that God made us in His own image. Students of the Bible have asked themselves for centuries what this means. Probably the simplest explanation is that God made us to be His representatives on earth.

1. What were the original responsibilities of the human race according to Genesis 1:26-28?

The human race was to manage and administrate God's world for Him in totally open communication with Him.

However, sin quickly destroyed this arrangement. The story of Jesus is the account of God's effort to restore the creation. There are many strong connections between the Gospels and the Old Testament, especially the creation story.

Genesis 5:1,2 states, "This is the book of the generations of Adam. In the day when God created man, He made him in the likeness of God. He created them male and female, and He blessed them and named them Man in the day when they were created."

Compare these verses to Matthew 1:1, the first verse of the New Testament: "The book of the generation of Jesus Christ" (KJV).

❓2. Why do you think Matthew made his first words so similar to Genesis 5:1,2?

❓3. How does Matthew 1:20-23 make the purpose of Christ's coming even clearer?

The Cultural Background to Christ's Coming

If you were to send someone an extremely important message spelling out the difference between life and death, you would want to make sure it was delivered accurately and understandably. God was infinitely more careful than we would have been in preparing the world for the coming of Jesus. Each of the three major cultures we see in the New Testament helped in significant ways to prepare the world for Christ's coming.

The Jewish Culture

God's first major step in restoring His fallen creation was to choose a specific people and culture to be the "landing place" where His Son would appear. He did this by calling Abraham, the ancestor of the Jewish people. (See Genesis 12:1-3.) The entire Old Testament describes how God led this nation into becoming the race of the Messiah. The Jewish culture prepared the world for Christ in the following ways:

Religion: The Jewish faith was the bright witness in the ancient world to the truth that there is only one God. The Jewish understanding of God from the Old Testament gave mankind the concepts necessary to interpret and apply Jesus' message and work.

Ethical and moral ideals: Though some of the individuals failed to live up to them, the Jewish people held the highest ethical ideals. For instance, they refused to kill newborn female babies, a practice common in the ancient world. Also, Jewish family life was a model for all other peoples in the Roman Empire. Furthermore, the Old Testament gave strong orders about the need to care for the poor and oppressed.

The synagogue system: The Jewish people had been scattered throughout the world after their various military defeats and exiles under successive conquerors. They formed communities and synagogues in almost every major city of the Empire. Traveling Jewish teachers went from city to city. This formed a natural communication network through which later Christ's undiluted message would spread quickly to the whole world.

The Greek Culture

The Greek culture also helped prepare mankind for Christ in three major ways:

Language and general education: Greek was spoken throughout the Empire. The early Christian missionaries could preach in Greek and be understood immediately. The New Testament was written later in the Greek spoken by ordinary citizens.

The importance of the individual: The Greeks had emphasized the importance of the individual for a long time in their writings and philosophy. This understanding was preserved and redeemed in the message of the gospel.

4. What did the apostle Paul tell the Christians, in the Greek seaport of Corinth, would happen to the individual who became a believer in Christ (2 Corinthians 5:17)?

THEREFORE IF ANY MAN BE IN CHRIST HE IS A NEW CREATURE: OLD THINGS ARE PASSED AWAY: BEHOLD ALL THINGS ARE BECOME NEW.

A spirit of thought and reflection: The Greeks developed an inquisitive attitude. As the philosophers of the ancient world, they paved the way for later work by Christian thinkers. This was the basis for Christian theology.

5. However, what extremes could the Greeks' inquisitive attitude lead to? See Acts 17:21. *AND TEACH CUSTOMS WHICH ARE NOT LAWFUL FOR US TO RECEIVE, NEITHER TO OBSERVE BEING ROMANS.*

The Roman Culture

The Romans were, of course, the rulers of the Empire. They contributed:

The "Pax Romana" or "peace of Rome": Augustus Caesar ended the bloody Roman civil wars and put down uprisings in the provinces. Roman political stability, even though it was built upon slavery and economic exploitation of the subject nations, enabled relatively unhindered preaching of the gospel.

Communications and travel: It was easier to travel in the days of Christ and the early church than at any time afterward, up until the middle of the nineteenth century. The Mediterranean Sea was clear of pirates for three hundred years.

Roman roads and transport facilities were the social arteries along which the message of Christ could flow.

Political and judicial system: The Roman provincial system of government created stability in society, and the Roman legal system held at least the ideal of justice. Persecutions of Christians did occur, but they were not terribly frequent.

🟄 6. What was the general attitude of the early Christians toward the Roman empire? Compare 1 Peter 2:12-14.

The Negative Side

On the other hand, each culture was in desperate need of Christ:

The Roman culture was becoming increasingly brutalized and corrupted by the economic exploitation of other nations and an all-pervasive preoccupation with war and conquering. Roman statesmen and leaders mourned the loss of old Roman values of industriousness and family, but they were powerless to stop the dry rot at the heart of their society.

The Greek culture had no solution for the problem of mankind's sin and guilt. The best philosophers had struggled to give morality a solid foundation, but had always failed to find an answer to the evil in the hearts of people. They lacked any bridge to a personal relationship with God. The old gods of the myths were long-dead, and the universe was an empty and lonely place for many thinking Greeks.

The Jewish culture was in danger of losing a personal relationship to God by creating a suffocating system of religious rules. There was also the problem of racism which cut the Jewish people off from true friendship with men and women of other cultures—the "Gentiles."

🟄 7.*According to Acts 10:28, what social rules did the

devout Jewish person have to observe in his contact with Gentiles?

? 8.*What effect did Christ's coming have on this division as far as His followers were concerned? See Ephesians 2:11-16.

The Purpose of the Four Gospels

This was the world into which Jesus, the Powerful Servant, came: a world prepared by God.

The records of His coming are preserved in the four Gospels. Two of these, Luke and John, state clearly why they were written.

Consider Luke's introduction in Luke 1:1-4.

? 9. How did Luke describe the people from whom he had gathered his material (verse 2)? EVEN AS THEY DELIVERED THEM UNTO US, WHICH FROM THE BEGINNING WERE EYEWITNESS AND MINISTERS OF THE WORD.

? 10. Why was he qualified to write this account (verse 3)? IT SEEMS GOOD TO ME ALSO HAVING HAD PERFELT UNDERSTANDING OF ALL THINGS FROM THE VERY FIRST, TO WRITE UNTO THEE IN ORDER, MOST EXCELLENT THEOPHILUS

? 11. What did he say his purpose was for writing (verses 3, 4)? THAT THOU MIGHTEST KNOW THE CERTAINTY OF THOSE THINGS, WHEREIN THOU HAST BEEN INSTRUCTED

? 12.*How does knowing the background to Luke's writing affect your confidence in the trustworthiness of the Gospels?

It is clear that the four evangelists had to be selective of their material when writing their books.

13. *How would you summarize the principle John says he used in collecting material for his book (John 20:30-31)?

AND MANY OTHER SIGNS TRULY RID JESUS IN PRESENCE OF HIS DISCIPLES, WHICH ARE NOT WRIT THIS BOOK 31 BUT THESE ARE WRITTEN, THAT YE MIGHT BELIEVE THAT JESUS IS THE CHRIST THE SON OF GOD; AND THAT BELIEVING YE MIGHT HAVE LIFE THROUGH HIS NAME.

APPLYING WHAT YOU'VE LEARNED

14. How has this study increased your appreciation for the way God prepared the world for the coming of His Son?

15. What specific changes do you want to see in your life through studying the life of Christ?

PRINCIPLES OF GOOD INTERPRETATION

We saw in this study that Luke and John clearly indicated their reasons for writing their Gospels. When we attempt to understand a book of the Bible, it is important to determine whether or not the author has told us directly or indirectly his reason for writing. This can help us correctly interpret his writing. Compare, for example, the explanation in Proverbs 1:1-6 of why that book was written.

STUDY 2
JESUS' BIRTH
AND CHILDHOOD

 ## INTRODUCTION

Imagine a play that is so long that it takes generations to act out. As the members of the cast grow old and die, their children take over their roles. It would be difficult for the players to understand the direction and purpose of the play unless the plot could be revealed to them.

Alfred Hitchcock, the famous filmmaker, wrote roles for himself into his film scripts. True Hitchcock fans watched for the moment when the familiar jowled figure would appear. The director became part of the plot. That is what the incarnation is all about. The Son of God, who had no history (after all, He made it!) stepped onto the stage of human life. As He walked and talked with the cast for thirty-three years, He gave us the key to understanding the whole story.

This is the startling claim of Christianity which sets it apart from all other religions: The author of everything has visited the earth. The incarnation is the central truth of the Christian faith. The Son of God came to us in human form, with flesh and bones, a mother, and normal human needs. He was burped like any other baby. He grew and learned how to speak and relate to other people. The idea is mind-boggling. As the New Testament puts it, "Great is the mystery of godliness: He was revealed in the flesh. . ." (1 Timothy 3:16)

The gospel writers handle the birth and boyhood of Jesus in different ways. Mark skips over the period entirely and begins his account with the appearance of John the Baptist. Matthew tells of the early period: Joseph's initial doubts, the story of the wise men, and the holy family's escape into Egypt and return to Nazareth. Luke presents the most detailed account of all, the visit of the angel to Mary and the birth of Jesus, while John reflects on the background in eternity to Jesus' coming.

In this study, we will concentrate our attention on Luke's account.

Jesus came as a servant—not as a ruler. He could have come to the family of the Roman Emperor or the Jewish High Priest. But He didn't. His family was so poor they could not scrape together enough money to buy the special lamb offering to celebrate His birth—and He was a firstborn son! That's pretty rough for a traditional Jewish family.

 LIFE PRINCIPLE: How to discover the importance of ordinary things in life.

Christ's incarnation bestowed great dignity on ordinary life. Home, school and work are not second-rate distractions;

they are the places where spiritual life should be rooted to reality.

In this study:

— You will discover the central importance of the incarnation for true Christianity.

— You will survey the gospel accounts of the birth and boyhood of Christ.

— You will think about areas of everyday life that need to be illuminated by the incarnation.

 INVESTIGATION

Read: Luke 1:26-2:52

AND IN THE SIXTH MONTH THE ANGEL GABRIEL WAS SENT FROM GOD UNTO A CITY OF GALILEE, NAMED NAZARETH

The Purpose of the Incarnation

Anselm of Canterbury, the famous philosopher of the middle ages, wrote an entire book about "Why God Became Man"; but the question arose long before Anselm. Why did God take such an unusual step?

1. Investigate the following texts and summarize briefly the reasons they give for the incarnation:

John 1:18 — *NO MAN HATH SEEN GOD AT ANYTIME. THE ONLY BEGOTTEN SON, WHICH IS IN THE BOSOM OF THE FATHER, HE HATH DECLARED HIM.*

Luke 1:30-33 — *AND THE ANGEL SAID UNTO HER FEAR NOT MARY: FOR THOU HAST FOUND FAVOUR WITH GOD AND, BEHOLD, THOU SHALT CONCEIVE IN THY WOMB, AND BRING FORTH A SON AND SHALT CALL HIS NAME JESUS.*

Luke 2:10,11 — *AND THE ANGEL SAID UNTO THEM FEAR NOT: FOR, BEHOLD, I BRING YOU GOOD TIDINGS OF GREAT JOY, WHICH GOOD TIDINGS OF GREAT JOY WHICH SHALL BE TO ALL PEOPLE.*

11 FOR UNTO YOU IS BORN THIS DAY IN THE CITY OF DAVID A SAVIOUR WHICH IS CHRIST THE LORD.

⑦ 2. According to John 1:1-3, what was Christ's position and work "before" the incarnation?

"Born of the Virgin Mary" — Luke 1:26-38

Luke goes to great length to record many of the circumstances surrounding Christ's birth. He seems to have had a special relationship to Mary, as he retells stories that must have grown out of her own recollections. His account of the appearance of the angel Gabriel to her is in Luke 1:26-38.

Mary is described as a young, unmarried girl engaged to a man named Joseph. In Palestine, engagements were commonly arranged by parents, sometimes for children as young as 12. An engagement usually lasted for about a year, and was as binding as marriage. But, even though the girl had the same legal status as a wife, it was not normal for intercourse to take place during that time.

The story of the virgin birth was not invented by Luke. Chapters 1 and 2 of Matthew provide an independent parallel. Both Gospels see Jesus' birth as a fulfillment of Isaiah's ancient prophecy (Isaiah 7:14), and attribute Christ's conception to the action of God. The story has all the earmarks of coming from the intimate circle of Jesus' family.

Through the centuries, Christians have honored Mary as the mother of the Lord, although they differ as to her importance.

⑦3.*How is Mary an example for us of genuine faith and obedience?

We often tend to focus our attention on Mary's role in the family life of Jesus, and rightly so. Yet, it must have taken an unusual man to marry such a woman and become the earthly father of our Lord.

4.*Study the following passages to discover the personal and spiritual qualities that made Joseph the man for the task of being the earthly guardian of our Lord:

Matthew 1:18, 19 —

Matthew 1:20-25 —

Matthew 2:13,14,19-23 —

Christmas — Luke 2:1-20

A very ancient tradition says that Jesus was born in a cave used to shelter animals in Bethlehem, a small town not far from the capital. Bethlehem's claim-to-fame was that it was "David's town," the birthplace and boyhood home of Israel's greatest king. One other thing distinguished Bethlehem from other villages. The prophet Micah had predicted that Messiah would be born there. But Jesus' family lived in Nazareth of Galilee. How was this hurdle to be overcome if Jesus truly were to be the promised redeemer?

The teachers of Israel had said long before that,

> The king's heart is like channels of water in the hand of the Lord; He turns it wherever He wishes.
>
> Proverbs 21:1

Luke 2:1-7 describes the events surrounding Christ's birth.

(?) 5. How do these events demonstrate the truth of Proverbs 21:1?

Luke goes on to describe the visit of a group of shepherds to the stable.

Bethlehem was a farm town. Because it was near Jerusalem, its economic life was linked to that of the capital. Sheep had been the primary livestock since David's time. Most of the flocks, though, would not have been kept in the open during the time Christmas is traditionally celebrated. However, there is one sheltered hollow near Bethlehem where they could have been out overnight. Some Bible scholars have speculated that these flocks kept out in the open fields were destined for sacrifice in the temple.

It is significant that the first "official" announcement of Christ's birth was made to ordinary poor people. From the very first, Jesus was especially close to the downtrodden and exploited.

The First Temple Visit — Luke 2:21-40

About a month after Jesus' birth, His parents brought Him to the temple to dedicate Him to God. The Old Testament law commanded the presentation of a burnt offering and a sin offering. Ordinarily, these would consist of a lamb and a dove or pigeon. If the people were poor, a bird could also be substituted for the lamb. The fact that Joseph and Mary chose this option shows their poverty. It is also a hint that the visit of the wise men came later. Otherwise Jesus' parents would have had sufficient funds to purchase a sacrificial lamb in the temple market.

Mary and Joseph met two remarkable people during this

visit, Simeon and Anna. Both were awaiting the promised redeemer.

❓6. According to Luke 2:25-27, what three things characterized Simeon's relationship to the Holy Spirit?

v.25 —

v.26 —

v.27 —

❓7. Do you think God still leads people as he did Simeon?

❓8. What spiritual disciplines were part of Anna's life (Luke 2:36-38)?

❓9. What place do you think these disciplines should have in our lives today?

The Visit of the Wise Men — Matthew 2

Matthew records the visit of a group of wise men, probably from Babylon.

Most Christmas pageants present the shepherds and wise men arriving at the same time. This is probably not accurate. Matthew pictures the holy family living in a house in the village, perhaps while Mary recovered from the birth or even longer. King Herod's butchering of all male children in the area under two years of age may hint at a longer interval. It was probably possible for a workman like Joseph to find employment in Bethlehem. He may even have considered settling there permanently (cf. Matthew 2:22), but God led the family back to Galilee and the North.

Jesus' Bar Mitzvah — Luke 2:41-52

Luke skips over the visit of the wise men and Egyptian flight. He describes the return of the holy family to Nazareth. He does not go into any detail about Jesus' early childhood. One is struck by the "down-home" simplicity of Christ's childhood. God gave simple human life a new dignity and glory by becoming man. Marriage and family, work and play, babies and children are not distractions from true spiritual life. They are where our spiritual life and growth has to take place, just as in Jesus' case. Our next glimpse into His development focuses on an incident when He was twelve years old. Jewish boys go through the Bar Mitzvah ceremony at this age to celebrate their entrance into manhood. At the age of 12 Jesus was already displaying great spiritual interest and insight.

❓10. What was unusual about the way the boy Jesus described His relationship with God (Luke 2:49)?

Luke twice mentions Mary's thoughtful reflection about incidents during Christ's boyhood (Luke 2:19; 2:51). But Luke also makes clear that Jesus' parents did not fully understand His relationship to God (Luke 2:50).

❓11.*Why do you think God allowed Jesus' parents to miss the significance of Christ's deity when He had made so many other things clear to both of them?

Many non-biblical stories about Jesus, written in the second century, contain wild and fanciful accounts of His boyhood. The Gospels leave a veil over these years, however, as well as over the eighteen years following his temple visit. Luke summarizes:

> He went down with them, and came to Nazareth; and He continued in subjection to them; . . . And Jesus kept increasing in wisdom and stature, and in favor with God and men.
>
> Luke 2:52

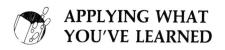 12.*Why do you think the gospel writers did not tell us more about Jesus' childhood?

APPLYING WHAT YOU'VE LEARNED

God put his final stamp of approval on our ordinary, everyday lives when He sent His Son to become man. Jesus, the Powerful Servant, did not spend the majority of His time doing things we would consider particularly "spiritual." Much of His time was taken up with ordinary things like working in Joseph's carpenter shop, eating with family or friends, walking or sleeping. He did not parachute out of heaven at thirty years of age. He was born and lived as a child. He had to learn, as we all do.

Yet, so often we think ordinary things like these are less spiritual than other, more "religious," activities. This is not so. It is in our everyday activities and concerns that our character and spiritual life are molded and shaped. How we respond to the pressures of finding money to pay the bills, final exams, or the irritation of a crying baby are tests of how genuine our spirituality is. How we respond to interruptions speaks volumes about our walk with God. Jesus lived through these things, too. They were the framework of His life with God.

❓ 13. What areas of your life do you have trouble relating to your faith?

❓ 14. Why are these areas such a difficult challenge for you?

❓ 15. What new steps do you want to take to tackle these responsibilities differently?

 ## PRINCIPLES OF GOOD INTERPRETATION

We saw in this study that the writers of the Gospels give no details about Jesus' early childhood and omit any description of the eighteen years after his Bar Mitzvah. Luke says simply, "When He began His ministry, Jesus himself was about thirty years of age" (Luke 3:23). This should tip us off to the fact that the Gospels are not "biographies" of Christ in the modern sense of the word. Their writers did not intend to give us a detailed description of the entire life and personal development of Christ.

What are the Gospels then? We must jump to the "end" of the story in order to begin to answer this question—to the resurrection. Matthew, Mark, Luke and John wrote under the massive impression left by the resurrection. They could not forget the fact that this man, Jesus, had died but then was raised from the grave and now is at God's right hand as Lord of all. The constant fact of the resurrection loomed over their lives like a massive peak in the Alps towers over a tiny Swiss village at its base. The Gospels are an attempt to give an explanation of how it came to pass that one man conquered death and sin. They are like a series of photos with commentary. They present the story with an explanation for those who could not be there or who never knew an eyewitness. We will never be able to answer all of our questions about Christ's life. The Gospels were not written for that purpose. They are a challenge to action, to actively place our faith in Jesus, the Powerful Servant, and to follow him for the rest of our lives. As the writer to the Hebrews put it,

> We must pay much closer attention to what we have heard, lest we drift away from it.
>
> Hebrews 2:1

STUDY 3
THE BAPTISM AND TEMPTATION

 INTRODUCTION

To the Jewish people the Old Testament stories were not dry-as-dust accounts of ancient times. Every week in the synagogue services the promises God gave to Abraham, Isaac, Moses and the other prophets were read aloud. Every Jewish child grew up knowing that God's acts in history were a pattern of how He was going to lead His people in the future. Every incident and every detail was studied with intense interest. History was the stage of God's work with His people and the Old Testament was the script.

One of the most important of these incidents was God's leading of Moses and the children of Israel out of Egypt and through the wilderness. The Jewish teachers explained that in the future the wilderness would once again play an important role when God would rescue His people from their oppressors once more. It was no accident that John the Baptist captured everyone's attention when he appeared in the wilderness and began preaching. Then, Jesus himself appeared and was baptized by John. The curtain was about to go up on the final, crucial phase of Jesus' life's work as the Powerful Servant of God.

 LIFE PRINCIPLE: How to have victory over temptation.

Jesus' baptism and temptation teach us that the only escape from temptation is to rely on God's Word and not on our own strength.

In this lesson:

— You will discover the biblical meaning of the term "gospel."

— You will study the significance of Jesus' baptism and temptation.

— You will learn from Christ's example how to deal with temptation in your own life.

 INVESTIGATION

Read: Mark 1:1-12

What Is the "Gospel"?

Mark begins his book with the words: "The beginning of the gospel of Jesus Christ, the Son of God." This is the title for his entire book.

"Gospel" or "good news" was a concept familiar to both pagans and Jews:

In the Roman or pagan culture it meant the joyful tidings

used to announce the festival days of the emperor's birthday, the coming of age of the crown prince, or the coronation of a new ruler.

In the Jewish culture the expression "gospel" came from the Old Testament, especially from the book of Isaiah.

? 1.*According to Isaiah 52:7, what is the content of the "gospel"?

? 2.*Jesus quoted another passage from Isaiah in Luke 4:17-21. According to verse 18, what does the gospel mean for the:

captives?

blind?

downtrodden?

The phrase, "the favorable year of the Lord," refers to the Old Testament law that ordered a year of "Jubilee" every 50 years in which all debts would be forgiven and social imbalances made right. Jesus said that His coming marked the beginning of God's great Jubilee, when God would open the way back to Himself and begin to restore the creation. This is the heart of the gospel.

John the Baptist

The last prophet of the Old Testament had predicted that, before God's promised kingdom would come, a prophet would appear like Elijah of old:

"Behold, I am going to send you Elijah the prophet
before the coming of the great and terrible day of the
Lord."

Malachi 4:5

God's prophets had often appeared in the wilderness area
in the south of Judah and east of the Jordan River.

The wilderness was a place of terrible heat, temptation,
and danger; but it was where God called His people and
personally led them. The wilderness was also a training
school for the prophets, especially Moses and Elijah. They
met God in the wilderness and received His word. This all
forms the background to the appearance of John the Baptist
on the scene.

3. According to Matthew 11:13,14, in what way did
John's arrival signal the end of one phase of God's plan for
mankind?

In the Gospel of John we read of John the Baptist's witness
for Christ.

4.*What two titles did he use to describe Jesus?

John 1:29 —

John 1:34 —

5.*Why do you think John used these titles—especially
the one in verse 29?

The Baptism of Jesus

Jesus' baptism is described in Mark 1:9-11.

Jesus did not need to repent and be baptized on account of His own sins (see John's confusion as reported in Matthew 3:13-15). He was baptized to identify Himself with God's people. Jesus' identification with the sinful people of Israel was similar to what Moses did in the wilderness after the Israelites had sinned by making themselves a golden calf as an idol. The story is told in Exodus 32:30-32.

God accepted Jesus' perfect repentance for His people just as He had that of Moses. This is shown by the heavens tearing open and the Holy Spirit descending on Jesus. The voice from heaven echoes Isaiah 42:1, but even more strongly Genesis 22:1, 2. Read these verses for background information.

In Judaism, Isaac was seen as the perfect picture of a beloved son and a willing sacrifice.

6.*In light of the Hebrew understanding of the story of Isaac, what do you think Jesus understood about His future work as God's Son when He heard these words from heaven?

The voice from heaven was a major factor in Jesus' understanding of His mission. The words of the Father helped Him deal with the shallow excitement of the crowds and leave them for the quiet of the desert or the sea. He knew what the real purpose of His coming was —and it was not to receive the cheap applause of the crowds.

The Temptation

After Jesus was baptized the Spirit would not allow Him

to leave the wilderness. He was tempted, and He struggled with Satan. This shed further light on what His life's task would involve: continuous confrontation with the enemy of men and God.

Read Matthew's account of this first encounter between Jesus and the devil in Matthew 4:1-11.

? 7. What is similar about the three replies Jesus made to Satan's temptations —in verses 4, 7 and 10?

? 8. How did temptation and continuing conflict with Satan emerge in Jesus' later work?

Mark 3:22-27 —

Mark 4:15 —

Mark 8:31-33 —

Mark 14:20, 21 (compare John 13:26, 27) —

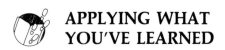 **APPLYING WHAT YOU'VE LEARNED**

The baptism and temptation of Jesus demonstrated His total obedience to the Father. He went into the wilderness and was baptized. He was willing to face temptation and conflict with Satan because the Spirit was leading Him.

Obedience is a prerequisite for victory in spiritual conflict.

❓9. In which areas of your life are you experiencing temptation or spiritual conflict?

❓10. What are you going to do to overcome this temptation?

PRINCIPLES OF GOOD INTERPRETATION

A writer will often set the stage for his entire book at the very beginning as Mark did. We should watch carefully for key themes at the beginning of a book which may then be repeated throughout the entire writing. For example, Jesus' conflict with Satan is a theme which appears frequently throughout Mark's Gospel.

STUDY 4
JESUS' EARLY MINISTRY

 INTRODUCTION

Jesus was different from the other teachers. At least that much was clear to those who watched His sudden rise to prominence as a traveling teacher in Israel. In this study we will be looking at exactly what it was that made Him different from the other rabbis who led the people of Judah and Galilee.

 LIFE PRINCIPLE: How to be a true disciple of Christ.

The heart of true discipleship is turning away from self-centeredness and submitting to the authority of Jesus in every area of life.

In this lesson:

— You will research the earliest period of Jesus' ministry by identifying key incidents from John's Gospel.

— You will investigate what the heart of Jesus' message was and why it made such an impact on those who heard Him.

— You will have the chance to evaluate your own activities to see if they reflect your priorities as a disciple.

 **INVESTIGATION**

Read: Mark 1:14-39

Jesus' Early Ministry in Judah

The first three Gospels—Matthew, Mark, and Luke—present the story of Jesus in much the same way. They view things similarly. Thus, they are called the "synoptic" Gospels. (From two Greek words meaning "together" and "seeing.")

The synoptic Gospels do not discuss the first formative period of Jesus' ministry. This early work, recorded in John 1-4, followed immediately after the baptism and temptation and took place in Judah and the southern areas of Palestine. John records the first contact of Andrew, Simon Peter and other disciples with Jesus during that time. Mark, on the other hand, starts with Jesus' radical call to "follow Me," which was based on those early encounters. Jesus seems deliberately to have avoided preaching in Galilee until after the imprisonment of John the Baptist. Matthew comments, "When He heard that John had been taken into custody, He withdrew into Galilee" (Matthew 4:12).

1. Investigate briefly John 1-4 and match the incidents listed below with the passages where they occur:

_____ John 1:19-34	A—Wedding at Cana
_____ John 1:35-51	B—Jesus visits Samaria
_____ John 2:1-12	C—John's witness at the baptism of Jesus
_____ John 2:13-25	D—Nicodemus visits Jesus
_____ John 3:1-21	E—Jesus meets His first followers
_____ John 3:22-36	F—Jesus cleanses the Temple
_____ John 4:1-42	G—John describes his work in relationship to Jesus
_____ John 4:43-54	H—Healing of a royal official's child

The Purpose of Jesus' Ministry

2. Summarize from Mark 1:14, 15:

What Jesus did (verse 14) —

The content of His message (verse 15) —

What man's response was to be (verse 15) —

3.*The key Old Testament passage concerning repentance during the time of Jesus was Hosea 14:1,2. Based on this passage what do you think repentance involves?

The radical nature of Jesus' work is seen in Mark 1:16-20. Jesus summoned four fishermen to follow Him. The incident highlights His authority and the proper response to it.

❓ 4. Analyze these verses from the following aspects:
   What did Jesus demand?

   What did Jesus promise?

   How did the men respond?

   With the call of these four men, Jesus began His program of calling people out of their self-centeredness and into new life. He summoned them to repent and believe. Just as God had once called the people of Israel out of Egypt, Jesus announced that the time had come for a new work of God —for a new exodus out of the slavery of sin and injustice. This says a lot about how far Israel had gone downhill. They were to be God's "chosen people," "Exhibit A" of how a society should be. But Israel had become enslaved spiritually and morally. The nation was a prison house of injustice propped up by religious piety. It was time for a new Exodus.

Jesus' Teaching

   Mark 1:21-39 describes *four incidents* which occurred during one or two days of Jesus' teaching in Capernaum, a town on the northern shore of the lake of Galilee. The province of Galilee was densely populated at that time. Josephus, the ancient Jewish historian, described the area: "The towns . . . are thickly distributed, and even the villages, thanks to the fertility of the soil, are all so densely populated that the smallest of them contains above fifteen thousand inhabitants" (*Jewish War*, III, iii, 3. Trans. by H. St. John Thackerey, Harvard Press).

   The *first incident* happened in the synagogue on the Sabbath.

? 5.*Review the story in Mark 1:21-28 and ask yourself, "What is Mark's main point about Jesus' teaching?" Note especially verses 22 and 27.

?6.*What was the striking difference between Jesus' teaching and that of the scribes?

?7. What was the reaction of the people?

Mark has placed this story at the beginning of his Gospel to underline clearly the full power and authority of Jesus. This brought Him again into open conflict with the power of darkness through a demon-possessed man. Christ did not find the man in a sleazy back-street bar in Capernaum. He was in the Synagogue. Apparently he was a respectable citizen. But he had given himself over to demonic power. The demon in control of the man's personality sensed a threat and challenged Jesus. Verse 24 means basically, "Why are you meddling and interfering with us?" But the defenses of the demon were powerless before Jesus. He silenced (muzzled) the unclean spirit, and ordered it to come out of the man.

At the time of the New Testament, exorcists used complicated chants and incantations to attempt to drive out demons. They usually appealed to the power of an angel to help them, and often used various herbs and medical potions to assist in the exorcism. Christ's absolute authority was clearly shown when the people saw that He did not use any magical manipulations to cast out the evil spirit. His word was authority enough.

❓8.*Jesus went with the four fishermen to Simon's house after the synagogue service. How does the *second incident* which occurred there further illustrate His authority (Mark 1:29-31)?

Mark 1:32-39 describes the *final two* of the four incidents. After a full day of preaching and healing by Jesus, the town crowded together to hear Him and to bring sick people to Him. He was surely tired and weary. He could have insisted upon His right to peace and quiet. But Jesus had come to serve. He was the Powerful Servant!

The following morning Jesus rose early and went outside the city to a deserted spot where He could pray alone. Jewish custom was to pray aloud. By leaving the village Jesus ensured His privacy and knew He would not disturb His sleeping friends. Only the very wealthy could afford homes with private bedrooms. In most homes, everyone— including guests—slept in the same room or on the flat roof during the hot summer months.

What is striking, though, is Christ's determination to leave Capernaum, the scene of obvious "success," and preach else-where. This was in spite of the fact that, as Peter said, "Every-one was looking for Him." He was seeking a much deeper response from the people than just superficial excitement about His miracles.

APPLYING WHAT YOU'VE LEARNED

Serving others means putting their interests ahead of our own. Being a disciple means, among other things, serving God through serving other people. This involves both our words and our actions. As disciples, we should talk to others about Christ. But we should know that they want to see our lives backup what we say.

9. What place does serving others have in your life?

10. Is your life balanced between telling others about Christ and showing them God's love in practical ways?

11. What changes are you going to make?

12. When are you going to do this?

Some practical steps might include attending a course on how to share your faith more effectively or becoming involved in practical activities in the community. You may decide to visit the sick, work for prison reform, or assist in medical or legal counseling centers.

 ## PRINCIPLES OF GOOD INTERPRETATION

It is helpful to break down a longer passage of Scripture into paragraphs to aid in understanding. Giving titles to these sections can aid in getting an overview of the contents. Many Bibles already have such divisions, and these can be used as a starting place for developing one's own titles.

This lesson also illustrates that an author can link various incidents together through the use of "time" or "place" words. Mark 1:21-39 links four sections together with expressions like "on the Sabbath" (v.21), "after they had come out of the synagogue" (v.29), "when evening had come" (v.32), and "in the early morning" (v.35). Such key words are important signals for understanding the course of events and the main points a writer is trying to get across.

STUDY 5
JESUS' CONFLICT
WITH RELIGION

 INTRODUCTION

In our last study we focused on the radical authority with which Jesus taught and acted. Mark's Gospel illustrates this by describing the calling of the fishermen and Jesus' authority over evil spirits and illness. However, Mark was also concerned to show that the people by and large did *not* fully obey the call to repentance and belief. They were content to use Christ's services as a miracle-worker or wonder-worker. This spiritual blindness characterized the people throughout Jesus' life.

But what of the spiritual leaders of the nation? Surely they would recognize Jesus' heaven-given authority and lead the people to follow Him? Tragically, this was not the case.

The religious authorities were as blind as the common people—and adamant in their opposition to Jesus. Jesus dramatically confronted the religious teachers of Israel and His absolute authority conflicted with their world view and social position.

Jesus' experience is important for His followers. His conflict teaches us the important principle that when one follows Jesus, it often means conflict with man-made religious systems.

 LIFE PRINCIPLE: How to handle conflict with man-made religion

Following Jesus often brings conflict with religious traditions.

In this lesson:

—. You will study a section of Mark's Gospel and analyze the heart of the conflict between Jesus and the religious leaders of society.

— You will expand your knowledge of *four groups* with whom Jesus had frequent contact: the scribes, the tax collectors, the Pharisees, and the Herodians.

— You will take time to reflect on your contact with those who do not yet know Christ, and think over how you can follow His example in your own life.

 **INVESTIGATION**

Read: Mark 2:1-3:6

Many passages in the Gospels speak of Christ's conflict with the religious leaders of Israel. In this study we will concentrate our attention on Mark 2:1-3:6. These verses contain stories which illustrate this conflict. It is unlikely that these incidents happened one right after the other, but Mark brought them together to make his point. These conflicts involved the religious establishment in Galilee, the northern region of the country.

🤔 1. Review the five incidents in Mark 2:1-3:6 and analyze the key issues of the conflict between Jesus and the religious leaders:

Mark 2:1-12 —

Mark 2:13-17 —

Mark 2:18-22 —

Mark 2:23-28 —

Mark 3:1-6 —

Let's examine each of these incidents more closely:

Mark 2:1-12

Jesus' word of forgiveness crystalized the opposition of the *scribes*. These were a closed guild of lawyers trained in interpreting and applying the written law of the Old Testament and the oral traditions of the Jewish teachers. Experts with long years of study behind them, the scribes had entered the guild through a special dedication ceremony. They influenced all aspects of Jewish life. They dominated religious practice through their open lectures and teaching in the synagogues. They were also called "lawyers," because they were responsible for the administration of the legal system as judges in the Sanhedrin, the supreme court of Israel and in local courts.

🅰2.*Why do you think the scribes became some of Jesus' most hardened opponents?

Blasphemy was the specific charge the scribes leveled at Jesus. They argued that Jesus claimed to forgive sins, which, according to the Old Testament, only God had the right to do. So they concluded that Jesus was a blasphemer.

Here are two passages in the Old Testament which attribute the power of forgiveness to God:

> I, even I [says God], am the one who wipes out your transgressions for My own sake; and I will not remember your sins.
>
> Isaiah 43:25

> Bless the LORD, O my soul... Who pardons all your iniquities and heals all your diseases.
>
> Psalm 103:2-3

🅰3. How is this similar to what Jesus did for the paralytic?

Sickness and death were not part of God's original plan for the human race. Scripture clearly teaches that sickness, disease, and even death are a result of mankind's rebellion against God. (Genesis 3 describes the beginning of this rebellion.) Some sicknesses may be due to specific sin in the life of an individual.

❓4. What is another possible reason for sickness, according to Jesus' statement in John 9:1-3?

Through his conversation with the paralytic, Jesus showed that we can be truly whole people only through a restored relationship with God. Jesus claimed the authority to forgive us and restore us to God's favor. Mark 2:10 summarizes: "The Son of Man has authority on earth to forgive sins."

Mark 2:13-17

Mark often pictures Jesus as withdrawing to a lonely region after demonstrating His saving power.

When Jesus challenged Levi, a despised tax collector, to follow Him, this brought Him into another conflict.

Tax collectors were used by the Roman occupation forces to squeeze various tax revenues out of the people of the occupied territories. Instead of having Roman officials collect customs taxes, salt tax, and other indirect and unpopular taxes, the imperial administrators employed local "tax farmers." The "tax farmers" were under contract to raise specific amounts of revenue and turn them over to the Romans. The tax collectors often took advantage of their position and lined their own pockets by charging more than the required taxes and keeping the difference. So they were a despised and hated class in Israel. Resentment of them was multiplied by the fact that they had to work on the Sabbath and had frequent contact with Gentiles. This made them ceremonially impure in the eyes of their fellow Jews. Therefore, they were not allowed to take part in many religious activities or hold office in the synagogues. The rabbis taught their own followers that they should not eat with such people.

⊘ 5.*How did Jesus justify His contact with people like the tax-gatherers (Mark 2:17)?

⊘ 6.*Do you think it would have been easy for you to eat with these people? Why or why not?

Mark 2:18-22

When Jesus lived, the strictest Pharisees went without food and drink on Mondays and Thursdays as an expression of their religious zeal. The disciples of John the Baptist probably fasted as an expression of repentance to bring the coming of redemption.

⊘ 7. With this background in mind, why was fasting inappropriate during the time Jesus was on earth?

Mark 2:23-28

⊘ 8. With which religious tradition did Jesus come into conflict in Mark's fourth incident?

The *Pharisees* were a group of devout laymen who had committed themselves to being absolutely faithful to the law of God and the traditions of Israel. They separated themselves from the common people whom they considered morally lax and irreligious. While the Sadducees came mainly from the class of wealthy landowners, the Pharisees attracted followers mostly from the ranks of skilled workers, shopkeepers and small businessmen. They tried to apply the customs and laws of Israel to everyday life by emphasizing the duty of each person to obey and fulfill the entire law of God. They believed that if every Israelite would keep the law for even one day, then Messiah would come and bring the kingdom of God to earth. To enable people to work toward this goal the Pharisees determined that the Old Testament contained a total of 613 commandments (365 negative, 248 positive). They then tried to develop rules for daily life which would prevent any possibility of anyone ever breaking them through ignorance or by accident. They called this "making a hedge" around the law.

The Pharisees emphasized external religious practices such as tithing and fasting and refused to eat in the homes of non-Pharisees in case the food were not ceremonially clean or had not been tithed. They had also developed a highly defined set of rules for the Sabbath which resulted in a very legalistic celebration.

❓9.*Why do you think the Pharisees became Jesus' enemies?

❓10. What did Jesus say was God's intention behind instituting the Sabbath?

? 11. How do you think God's original intention can apply to society today, even though most people do not celebrate the Sabbath?

Mark 3:1-6

In his fifth story Mark brings the tension to a climax as he reports on a healing that Jesus performed on a Sabbath in a synagogue somewhere in Galilee. The main focus of these verses is not on the healing but on the conflict between the Master and His opponents, during which He silenced them with His pointed question.

The oral tradition of the rabbis stated that even good deeds, such as healing, which could be done on the Sabbath should wait unless someone's life was in danger. Jesus saw clearly that this violated one of God's main intentions in establishing the Sabbath—the healing and restoration of life through rest and quiet.

When Jesus failed to submit to their tradition, the Pharisees and scribes made a fatal assumption. They assumed that disrespect for their tradition was disrespect for the Scripture itself. This led to their rejection of Jesus.

Verse 6: The *Herodians* were associated with the puppet government of Herod Antipas. Most came from the landed nobility, the economic and political establishment committed to the status quo.

12. Since the religious customs of the Pharisees probably meant little to the Herodians, what reasons could they have had for allying themselves with them against Jesus?

This study closes with storm clouds on the horizon. Not only did the common people fail to obey Jesus' call, but the official religious leaders of the nation had concluded that the Messiah, the bearer of salvation, did not fit into their tradition and had to be eliminated (see Mark 3:6). The guardians of God's law were preparing to commit murder to protect their status!

 ## APPLYING WHAT YOU'VE LEARNED

One great difference between true followers of Jesus and those playing "religion" should be apparent in their attitudes toward outsiders. Jesus was willing to endure the misunderstanding of the influential in order to help social outcasts and those far away from God. He expects His followers to display the same love and openness to those who are not yet Christians.

In Mark 2:15-17 Jesus gave us an example of how one could do this.

13. With whom would you like to share your faith in Christ?

🔹14. What two or three concrete steps do you want to take to help that person see Christ more clearly?

🔹15. When are you going to put these steps into action?

 **PRINCIPLES OF GOOD INTERPRETATION**

In this lesson we discussed some of the groups Jesus confronted in his lifetime: the scribes, the tax collectors, the Pharisees, and the Herodians. This kind of information can be found in a Bible dictionary, and is important to your understanding of the Bible. A Bible dictionary is especially useful for:

— a first "overview" of a book of the Bible or a subject one is beginning to read or study;

— explanation of words, terms, or customs with which one may be unfamiliar.

Good Bible dictionaries have lists of important books or articles for further in-depth study of a subject. A book of this type should be one of the first purchases one makes for serious study.

Two of the best are:

The New Bible Dictionary, ed. J. D. Douglas, Wheaton: Tyndale Press, 2nd ed., 1982.

The Illustrated Bible Dictionary, 3 Vols., ed. Norman Hillyer, Wheaton: Tyndale Press, 1980.

STUDY 6
THE APPOINTMENT
OF THE APOSTLES

 ## INTRODUCTION

Jesus' spiritual program was His summons of men and women to repent and believe in the good news of the Kingdom. His method centered on twelve people, whom He called to follow Him. He sent them out to take His message to others. We are often inclined to think that new methods or techniques are needed for spiritual awakening, but Jesus placed His emphasis on twelve ordinary people. As E. M. Bounds once said, "The church is looking for better methods; God is looking for better men." The strategy of Jesus reveals the principle of concentrating on people and not programs.

The "Twelve" are a major theme of all of the gospel

accounts. Jesus consciously multiplied His ministry through the calling and training of these apostles. In the midst of growing spiritual darkness among the people and their national leaders He called the Twelve to carry the light. He devoted His major effort to making them into the people they would need to be in order to represent Him in the world.

The continuing spiritual blindness of the crowds and the growing conflict with the religious authorities and even with His own family formed an undercurrent of tension in Jesus' situation. His mission did not go unopposed. Nevertheless, He concentrated His attention on the Twelve. They were not spiritual supermen. Yet, He knew that you can't change crowds. You can only change individuals. Jesus' concern was to find the individual out of the mass who would begin to follow Him even though things were not one hundred percent clear and understandable. Christ was not demanding perfection, but availability. He was committed to unfolding the possibilities that were in those men! Trying to do that in a crowd would have been like hunting rabbits with a brass band. He was not interested in merely influencing people. He wanted to change them and enlist them for God's kingdom—to be God's servants in the world. This meant they had to be willing to identify with Him—even to the point of suffering.

 LIFE PRINCIPLE: How to serve Christ.

Jesus does not call perfect people to serve Him. He wants us to come to Him just as we are—with a willing heart. He wants us to follow Him. He will take care of our inadequacy.

In this lesson:

— You will discover why Jesus concentrated His efforts on twelve ordinary people to whom He later entrusted His message for the world.

— You will consider the reasons why Jesus often commanded people not to make Him known.

— You will apply what you have learned about following Jesus by diagnosing your own attitude toward suffering.

 INVESTIGATION

Read: Mark 3:13-35

The Unbelief of the Crowds

The crowds continued to follow Jesus as a "wonderworker," but they showed no response to His call for repentance and faith. They seem to have wanted only physical healing and did not understand Him or His mission.

There was only one group that recognized Christ's true identity. That was the demons!

> Whenever the unclean spirits beheld Him, they would fall down before Him and cry out, saying, "You are the Son of God!" And He earnestly warned them not to reveal His identity.
>
> Mark 3:11,12

Why did Jesus give the command not to make Him known?

In the synoptic Gospels, especially in Mark, Jesus silenced the demons when they tried to cry out His identity to the crowds. But Jesus went even further. He would often not permit those who were following Him to trumpet about His power to perform miracles or His identity. (Compare Mark 5:43; 8:29,30; 9:9,10.) Some critics have said this is a literary invention of Mark which they claim he developed to give his own interpretation to the gospel story. But, there is a better explanation.

It is clear to us that for Jesus to be the Messiah and the Son of God He must go to the cross. We know the end of the gospel story. But that is precisely the reason why Mark and the other writers told the story: the person of Christ can only be understood with the cross in the middle of the picture. Jesus was not just a "miracle man"—a sort of Superman figure who darted about doing wonder-healings and exorcisms. He was above all the Suffering Servant of God.

Mark shows that any understanding of Jesus, the Powerful Servant, has to be rooted in the Old Testament, with the cross and the resurrection in the center of the picture. In light of this, the reason for Jesus' silencing the demons and warning his followers to "keep things quiet" becomes clear: the demons were promoting a false picture of His work through their acclamations. They were proclaiming a "son of God" without the cross. This was the center of the devil's repeated temptations of Jesus: He was trying to persuade Christ to abandon the road of suffering and become the "successful" Messiah the people expected. The crowds would have become even more enthusiastic if Christ had not silenced the demons. The excitement and enthusiasm of these people was not based on repentance and faith but on what they thought Jesus could do for them. To preach Jesus without the cross and the resurrection is to side with the demons! And any picture of discipleship that leaves out sharing in the suffering of Christ is demonic.

The Calling of the Twelve

Review Mark's account of this in Mark 3:13-19.

Mark makes a special point of emphasizing the mountain which Jesus climbed.

❓1. Does any important passage of the Old Testament

come to mind that Mark might be hinting at? (Glance through the book of Exodus if you need help.)

2. What additional light does Luke 6:12 shed on Jesus' reason for ascending the mountain?

3.*Why do you think it was important for Jesus to retreat to the mountains at the time He was about to call his disciples?

4. Identify the four characteristics of an apostle as listed in Mark 3:14,15:

(1) *Appointed by Jesus* (v.14)_____

(2) _____ (v.14)_____

(3) _____ (v.14)_____

(4) _____ (v.15)_____

One New Testament scholar made a profound observation about the qualifications Jesus was looking for in these men:

"Included in their training was instruction about the demands involved in discipleship. Instead of confronting these men at the time of their call with a formidable list of conditions they must meet in order to serve under Him, Jesus sought in them a willingness to follow Him" (Everett

Harrison, *A Short Life of Christ,* Grand Rapids, MI: Eerdman's, 1968, p.146).

❓5.*How should this fact influence the way we present following Christ to those who do not yet know Him?

Jesus was planning for the future when He chose these men. Their selection and training are evidence that He was thinking of the church that He would build.

❓6. What role did Paul say in Ephesians 2:19-21 the apostles had played in the establishment of the church?

Jesus' True Family

The Twelve and Jesus' other followers became the core of a new society. They were the beginning of a new humanity. At the same time, others reacted negatively to His message, including His own family.

❓7. How would you summarize the accusation made against Jesus by His family in Mark 3:20,21 and the reason they had come to this conclusion?

That this accusation by Jesus' family is mentioned at all in the New Testament demonstrates the great integrity of the gospel writers. They faithfully recorded the material and reports they had received. Writers who played fast and loose with their subject matter would never have included such an incident.

More Conflict with the Scribes: Mark 3:22-30 and 31-35

Mark has divided the account of Jesus' conflict with His family into two sections.

8. This writing technique can serve three functions:
_____ (1) It can indicate a lapse of time.
_____ (2) It can heighten the tension for the reader.
_____ (3) It can focus attention on parallels or contrasts.

Why do you think Mark divided verses 20,21 from their conclusion in verses 31-35? Put a check beside the functions listed above when you think they explain why Mark wrote this way.

9. What two charges did the scribes make against Jesus in verse 22?

(1)

(2)

Christ reacted to these accusations with firm rebukes and a solemn warning:

> Truly I say to you [other translations say "Amen, Amen"], all sins shall be forgiven the sons of men, and whatever blasphemies they utter; but whoever blasphemes against the Holy Spirit never has forgiveness . . . (verses 28,29)

This is the first use of "Amen, amen" or "Truly I say to you" in the Gospel of Mark. It appears twelve more times in Mark. At the time of Jesus, it was common for Jewish teachers to use this expression to show their agreement with the statement of another person. Jesus, however, used this formula to introduce His own words—a revolutionary claim!!

Jerome, who translated the Bible into Latin, commented on this phrase, "'Amen, amen, I say to you' in the New Testament is the equivalent of 'As I live saith the Lord' in the Old Testament."

Many sensitive people have been frightened by reading Jesus' warning about the sin against the Holy Spirit. They fear they have committed this sin, for which there is no forgiveness. Note carefully, though, the following points:

— This sin is described specifically in the Bible. It involves attributing the work of Christ during His ministry on earth to the power of demons.

— The sin against the Spirit is not just a one-time verbal statement but a consistent and repeated attitude and accusation: "They were saying..." (habitually and repeatedly as an expression of their hostility toward Jesus.)

— Anyone who is worried about this sin has not committed it! Anyone who had so hardened his heart as to have fulfilled the first two "conditions" would be immune to the Holy Spirit's convicting power. He would not be concerned about having committed this sin.

Verses 31-35 conclude the story about Jesus' family.

10.*According to these verses, who is the genuine "family" of Jesus?

11.*When followers of Jesus are persecuted by *their* families, what assurance does Mark 3:31-35 hold for them?

Jesus consistently paid high regard to family obligations. (Compare Mark 7:9-12.) However, when these obligations were used in an attempt to water down His radical call to discipleship, He made clear where a person's priorities must lie.

APPLYING WHAT YOU'VE LEARNED

The apostle Paul wrote that we have fellowship with Christ through suffering. This is an honor for the believer, according to Philippians 1:28. Yet, many people today who want to follow Jesus are unwilling to suffer with Him. This is not the discipleship of the first Christians.

12. How have you suffered for Christ?

13. What changes do you need to make in your attitude toward suffering as a Christian?

14. Is there any area of your life that keeps you from following Jesus wholeheartedly, even to the extent of suffering for Him?

❓15. What specific changes do you want to make in these areas in order to be a more consistent disciple?

 ## PRINCIPLES OF GOOD INTERPRETATION

Using a "synopsis": Often in studying the Gospels, one wants to compare the accounts written by the different authors. A Bible study tool that saves time when one wants to do such parallel studies in the Gospels is called a "synopsis." This is an arrangement of the Gospels, usually the first three, so that the parallel passages can be easily compared. Synopsis, as we saw in an earlier study, comes from two Greek words meaning "seeing together." These arrangements are useful for quickly comparing the accounts in different Gospels of an event in the life of Christ.

However, it is important to realize that each writer recorded details and arranged his material somewhat differently from the others. Luke, for example, rearranged the order of the temptations in his account of Jesus' confrontation with Satan. Luke probably did this in order to emphasize the outcome of the struggle in the Temple. This causes no difficulty. Every author has that kind of freedom to present his material. But in some cases we simply lack enough information to fit the accounts together. In such instances it is wise to leave the issue until further studies shed more light on the passage. The difficulties in reconciling the accounts of the life of Christ are not overwhelming. Christians have recognized the basic questions for centuries and the underlying historical accuracy of the Gospels is not clouded by these questions.

STUDY 7
THE PURPOSE OF PARABLES

 **INTRODUCTION**

Most people know that Jesus taught in parables; but if one were to ask the average person to define parables and state their purpose, he would have trouble answering.

For most of us the parables are interesting "stories" Jesus told about seeds and birds, vineyards and Samaritans. Why He used them in His teaching may be unclear in our minds.

But we can discover the key to Jesus' parables and their purpose if we carefully study their connection to the heart of Jesus' message: the Kingdom of God. The Gospels include a great deal of material on the subject. Matthew, for instance, focuses the entire Sermon on the Mount (Matthew 5-7) around the Kingdom. Jesus' teaching about the Kingdom of God is a guideline for us as His disciples. He is not simply concerned to save our souls for heaven, He wants to establish God's rule over our daily lives and relationships.

There is a dynamic tension in Jesus' teaching about the Kingdom: on the one hand, the Kingdom has already come; on the other, Jesus points to a future time when it will be here in completion and glory. This tension is a reflection of two Old Testament themes: God is King and Lord of the earth right now—and yet the day is still to come when He will finally return to set up His personal rule. We live our lives in tension between these two poles: "already" and "not yet." The King has come, but in disguise, not openly. He has set up God's underground—composed of those men and women who trust Him. They comprise the core of His present Kingdom. As His disciples, we are to live in total obedience to Him in the Power of his Spirit, within the standards He set up. Our lives are to become a living demonstration of what would happen if God ruled every human heart on earth, as He will when King Jesus returns.

Jesus said, "You are the salt of the earth . . . you are the light of the world." Salt preserves from decay. Light exposes and drives out darkness. Recent research in England has shown that when Christians are actively involved in the social and political life of their town, the entire quality of life in the area is significantly higher than elsewhere. It is our job as Jesus' people to speak of Him with our lips and back up this testimony with our lives.

 LIFE PRINCIPLE: How to begin to understand the secrets of God's Kingdom.

Commitment comes before understanding in God's economy. God is unwilling to reveal the truth to someone who is just theoretically interested in following Christ. Jesus remains a riddle until one is prepared to commit himself to the truth he discovers.

In this lesson:

— You will develop a basic understanding of how to interpret parables correctly.

— You will recognize why Jesus taught in parables.

— You will have a chance to clarify your thinking about God's kingdom and interact with a tension created for Christians by the truth that Christ will return again.

 **INVESTIGATION**

Read: Mark 4:1-34

There are numerous parables in the Gospels, but many are clustered thickly in Matthew 13, Mark 4, and Luke 13-16. We will concentrate our attention, as we have in the past studies, on Mark's material.

1. How would you title the four parables in Mark 4:1-34?

_____: verses____to____

_____: verses____to____

_____: verses____to____

_____: verses____to____

Jesus explained through these parables why people did not always believe His message. He pointed out that they have different motives which predetermine their response to the Word of God. This response in turn determines how much they really understand Him and His message. The crowds "heard" His message, but did not truly apply it to themselves. The disciples, on the other hand, were eager to receive more truth, although they had not yet reached the point where they applied all of what they were hearing to their own personal lives. However, because of their eagerness, Jesus was prepared to explain and reveal more truth to them. By including such parables in the Gospels, the writers illustrated what Jesus meant when He spoke of the Kingdom of God. His coming is a mystery: the King has come to His world, but only those who are willing to commit themselves to Him understand His true identity. His coming began the process which will culminate in the triumph of God's purpose for the human race.

Mark 4:1-2 — The Setting

Mark describes the setting of this passage. Jesus was sitting in a boat by the lake shore, teaching the people gathered on the beach. Mark 4:1-34 may well be a summary of His teaching to the crowds. In verse 2 Mark states that this is only a fragment of a longer sermon.

Mark 4:3-20 — First Parable

The first parable in Mark 4 begins with the challenge to listen carefully. Parables were not just preaching illustrations but stories which required attentive hearing. This parable occupies a key position in each of the first three Gospels. (Compare Matthew 13 and Luke 8.) It is Jesus' explanation of the different responses to His message.

Cultural background: To understand this parable correctly, it is important to know the difference between plowing practices in the Palestine of Jesus' day and those of our day: Today *plowing* precedes *sowing;* then comes growth and harvest. In Jesus' day, however, the seed was scattered and then plowed into the ground. *Sowing* came first, then *plowing,* followed by growth and harvest.

The sower was not being careless in where he threw the seed; he was willing to scatter the seed everywhere, knowing that the plow would turn it under and enable growth to start.

Two things in the parable attract our attention:

The *seed* and the *sower*

The seed was specifically defined by Jesus as the Word, the good news of God as defined in Mark 1:15,16—the proclamation of peace and salvation under the rule of God.

? 2.*As you reflect on our studies to this point, whom do you think the sower represents?

The principle of this parable applies to any situation where "sowing" of the gospel takes place. We who follow Christ should sow widely in order to reap a bountiful harvest.

? 3.*Compare the parable itself (vs.3-8) with the interpretation (vs.14-20). Fill in the following diagram to help in making the comparison:

Four Soil Types	Fate of Seed	Response to Word	Interpretation
1. *along the path*		*Just Hear it.*	
2.	*grows up - then withers*		
3.			*Never fruitful or mature*
4.			

🤔 4. Do you know individuals who have reacted to the message of Christ in these different ways?

Mark 4:21-25 — Second Parable

These sayings have been brought together by Mark because of their relevance to Jesus' teaching through parables. They occur in separate places in the other Gospels.

🤔 5. Mark 4:21 literally says: "Does the lamp come." To what do you think Jesus was referring by the image of the lamp?

🤔 6. Why do you think He chose this image? Compare John 1:6-9.

In verses 24,25, Christ's call to decision is expanded by the image of the measure. It is an appeal for spiritual insight and faith in Jesus' word. There are two pictures used:

The measure: Whatever one gives his attention to now is the standard that determines participation in God's kingdom in the future.

Possessions: Whatever one has now determines what he will receive in the Kingdom.

The central requirement for participation in the Kingdom of God is faith. The person who hard-heartedly refuses to receive the Word NOW will experience acute loss LATER. How one responds to the Sower now will determine his reception by the Harvester then.

Mark 4:26-29 — Third Parable

This little parable is unique to Mark. It contrasts with the parable of the Sower in what it focuses on:

PARABLE OF SOWER:	PARABLE OF SEED GROWING:
	Sowing
	Growth Opposition
	Progress

⊗7. What do you think Jesus was emphasizing through this parable?

"All by itself the soil produces grain" (verse 28).

This statement stresses the fact that the seed does not depend on human intervention for its growth. God's Kingdom will come. The seed has been sown and the day of harvest is mysteriously but irresistibly drawing nearer as the seed grows to maturity.

Mark 4:30-32 — Fourth Parable

This parable reminds us that the day will come when God's Kingdom will be more splendid than the mightiest kingdoms of earth. Although the mustard seed was called proverbially the "smallest of all seeds" by the rabbis, the mustard plant grew sometimes to a height of fifteen feet! (Its normal height was about four feet.)

Mark 4:33-34 — Why Jesus taught in Parables

As background, read again Mark 4:10-12.
Jesus said that the "mystery" or "secret" of the Kingdom

of God was given to the disciples and not to those on the outside.

Verses 33,34 must be understood in light of the incidents of opposition to Jesus that we studied in previous lessons. Unbelief and hatred of His work were open for all to see. Surrounded by such a tension-filled atmosphere of resistance, Jesus made a sharp distinction between the disciples and the unbelieving crowd. Both groups "saw" and "heard" Him, but there was a dramatic difference in their understanding.

The response of the disciples and the response of the crowd can be illustrated by the following sketch:

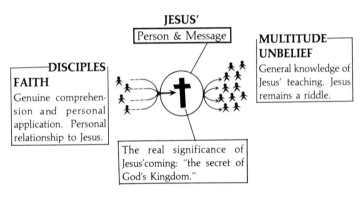

8.*With this in mind, what is your first impression as to why Jesus taught in parables?

Whenever Jesus enters the human scene, His coming produces either acceptance or rejection. His coming is a puzzle to those whose hearts are closed. His mission and His identity are a "parable" to them. Those whose eyes are blinded and ears dulled recognize nothing in Jesus but a disturbing enigma. Unbelief makes Him and His message a riddle. The disciples, on the other hand, began to know the secret of the Kingdom of God: its arrival in the person of the King.

Mark 4:12 quotes from the Old Testament prophet Isaiah (Isaiah 6:9,10):

> . . . in order that while seeing, they may see and
> not perceive; and while hearing, they may hear and
> not understand lest they return and be forgiven.

Jesus' teaching in parables was a judgment on unfaithful Israel just as Isaiah's ministry was. The parables hid the truth about God's purpose from the hardhearted and disobedient people who refused to repent, believe and become disciples. The blindness of the crowd was an illustration of this Old Testament prophecy. Their lack of understanding was due to their unbelief.

These verses do not teach that those "outside" are denied the possibility of belief. However, it does teach that they are prevented from understanding as long as their unbelief continues.

9. What does this prophecy (v.12) say would happen if the crowd would give up its unbelief?

10. Read Luke 7:30, which describes the unbelief of the scribes and Pharisees. Who was responsible for their not experiencing God's purpose and plan for their lives?

⑨11. According to Luke, what would they have had to do to experience God's purpose for themselves?

⑨12.*What does Mark 4:33,34 imply was Jesus' real reason for using parables to teach the crowd?

The key to the Kingdom is a believing heart. Those whose hearts are hard are not forced to believe. But each person must make a decision about Christ. Not until the final harvest of the ages will the true significance of Jesus be clear for all people to see.

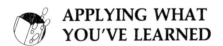 ## APPLYING WHAT YOU'VE LEARNED

God's kingdom is not something we can bring about by our own effort. Each day as we pray, "Thy kingdom come, Thy will be done on earth as it is in heaven" we express our dependence upon God to bring final justice and change to this earth.

We *receive* the Kingdom as little children by giving our allegiance to Jesus (Mark 10:15).

We *illustrate* the Kingdom by reflecting God's love, character, and justice (See 1 Peter 2:11,12).

We *proclaim* the Kingdom to others in the gospel, as the apostles once did (See Acts 20:25).

But we cannot "make" the Kingdom happen. That will take place when the King returns. In the meantime, though, we are to be God's underground, living in obedience to him as dynamic illustrations of the lifestyle and values of His kingdom.

There is a creative tension in our lives parallel to the tension we have noticed in the New Testament:

We are to be living models of God's rule over the world. This was why He created the world. Emphasizing this points us toward settling down, taking care of the earth, establishing and preserving justice and peace, and fitting into His plan of marriage and family unless He calls one to singleness.

On the other hand we are to live unencumbered, as though Christ were returning tomorrow, and proclaim His gospel with every ounce of energy and every resource available.

The following incident, which actually occurred, is an example of how this tension can express itself. See what you think:

A group of sugar farmers who are committed Christians recently came to an older believer and said, "As you know, we have large sugar plantings. Sugar can 'burn out' the soil if grown constantly on the same land for too long. But, since Christ is returning soon and the gospel must be preached to all people, we've decided to 'burn out' our land for the next ten or fifteen years and give the profits we'll make for missionary work. What do you think? Are we doing the right thing?"

🕐 13. How would you counsel these believers?

🕐 14. How do you experience this tension in your own life?

🌓15. What are you going to change in your life to deal better with this tension?

 ## PRINCIPLES OF GOOD INTERPRETATION

Parables are truth expressed through concrete pictures. The word "parable" can refer to all kinds of figurative forms of speech, but most parables are expended illustrations. Because details are necessary simply to paint a word picture, many specific details in parables are not to be interpreted. They are just part of the scenery. A parable should not be overinterpreted!

Parables are an emotional and concrete appeal to take a stand and decide. They stimulate the imagination, pull the hearer into the action, and challenge him or her to apply what is heard to the individual situation. The parables are about Jesus, His coming, and His mission, and NOT about some exotic teaching. One must always ask, "How does this parable relate to Christ?"

Parables also usually center around the Kingdom. They explain what the Kingdom is like in the age in which we live during the absence of the King. Many parables also point toward the time when He will return. Nevertheless, parables should not be used on their own to build doctrines about the end time. Clear teaching passages of the New Testament should be the foundation for any such doctrine. The parables were not given as lectures in theology but as calls to a changed life and obedience to the gospel. Thus, we should beware of reading too much into the parables about the nature of God's program for the end time.

STUDY 8
JESUS' POWER

 INTRODUCTION

After presenting parables about the Kingdom of God,
all the synoptic Gospels bring a series of stories illustrating
the power of Jesus. A turning point had come in Christ's
life and work. The crowd ignored His call to repentance
and faith, and the religious leaders resisted His authority.
Only those who had left all to follow Him had even a
glimmer of understanding about His work or His true
identity. Most of the crowd probably applauded Him as
a traveling wonder-worker. He was much more than that,
though, regardless of what the crowd thought.

It is at this point that all four gospel writers chose to illustrate more clearly just who Jesus is and what the proper

response to His authority is. We will again center our attention on Mark's account. Parallel passages are in Matthew 8:18-9:26 and Luke 8:22-56.

In Mark 4:35-5:43 two main themes stand out:

— The person of Jesus: "Who is this, that even the wind and the sea obey Him?" The answer to the question is shown by Jesus' power over natural elements and human experience.

— The proper response to Him: "Why are you so timid? How is it that you have no faith?" The question is, "What does true faith in Christ involve?"

 LIFE PRINCIPLE: How to make progress in the Christian life.

True discipleship progresses from an early stage—when we focus on what Jesus, the Powerful Servant, can do for us—to a life centered on Him personally. He Himself becomes much more important than what He can do.

In this lesson:

— You will learn about Jesus' power over things that can mold and even destroy your life.

— You will discover characteristics of true faith.

— You will have the opportunity to meditate on some concrete steps you can take to help your faith grow.

 **INVESTIGATION**

Read: Mark 4:35-5:43

❓1. Give a title to the following paragraphs:

Mark 4:35-41 — Christ's power over _____

Mark 5:1-20 — Christ's power over _____

Mark 5:21-43 — Christ's power over _____

(?) 2.*These stories teach us much about Jesus' use of his power. What released his power in the following situations?

During the storm (Mark 4:38) _____

A demon possession (Mark 5:2-8) _____

The encounter with Jairus (Mark 5:23) _____

The encounter with the sick woman (Mark 5:27,28, 34)

_____

Mark 4:35-41: _____ (Fill in your paragraph title.)

After a long day of teaching and healing, Jesus suggested to the disciples that they depart from the area and go to the opposite side of the lake. If, as early church tradition states, Mark was Peter's assistant, this account probably comes directly from the apostle.

(?) 3. In this passage are many details that are "unnecessary" to the plot and point to an eyewitness account. Briefly list some of these "extra details":

(?) 4. Review the following Old Testament passages and

summarize what the Hebrews believed about the control of wind and weather:

Psalm 65:5-7 —

Psalm 89:9 —

Psalm 107:23-32 —

⍰ 5.*What does Mark 4:39 tell us about how Jesus viewed His own authority?

> He said to them, "Why are you so timid? How is it that you have no faith?" (verse 40).

Rebuke and correction are essential to a life of discipleship. This is the first in a series of rebukes which Jesus gave the disciples. Correction is an integral part of spiritual growth, yet the process of correction is almost a forgotten part of the Christian life today.

⍰ 6.*Why do you think correction and rebuke are such neglected features of our relationship to one another as modern Christians?

Mark skillfully ends this section with the question the disciples asked in the boat:

Who then is this, that even the wind and the sea obey Him? (verse 41)

7. What answer do you think Mark was looking for from the reader?

Mark 5:1-20 — _____ (Paragraph title)

A tragic result of nineteenth-century materialism is its lasting influence on Christians. Many believers are embarrassed by the biblical accounts of demons because they believe modern psychology has proven that the people involved were simple mentally ill. Although mental illness was one result of demon possession, much more was involved. As a matter of fact, the biblical writers themselves recognized the difference between demonic influence and neurological disorders such as epilepsy. (See for instance, *Christian Counseling and Occultism* by Kurt Koch, Grand Rapids: Kriegel Publications for further information.)

8. What are the various categories of suffering described in Matthew 4:24?

Satan's goal is the distortion and destruction of the human personality as the "image-bearer" of God. In the case of demon possession the center of the personality is influenced by alien powers which seek to ruin the person and sometimes drive him to self-destruction. The ego is so suppressed that the spirits speak through him.

9. Contrast the situation of the demon-possessed man

before and after his encounter with Jesus:

BEFORE (Mark 5:3-5)	AFTER (Mark 5:15-20)
Living situation —	
Social relations —	
Appearance —	
Personal actions —	

A note as to the location of this incident:

This encounter did not take place at the city of Gerasa, 30 miles southeast of the lake, but near the modern Kersa on the eastern shore. William Lane writes in his commentary,

> At the site of Kersa, the shore is level and there is a fairly steep slope within forty yards from the shore, and about two miles from there cavern tombs are found which appear to have been used for dwellings. (William Lane, *Commentary on the Gospel of Mark*, Grand Rapids: Eerdmans, 1973, p. 181).

❓10. How does what happened to the swine help us understand Satan's goal in demon possession?

?11. How would you answer if someone were to argue: "What about the poor pigs and their owners? Wasn't it wrong of Jesus to allow such a thing to happen?"

Mark 5:21-43 — _____ (Paragraph title)

Since mankind first rebelled against God, sickness and death have been our common experience. Jesus came to destroy sin's grip on mankind and ultimately to abolish even death. Thus, the two incidents reported in this section clearly illustrate the meaning of Christ's coming.

We must keep in mind that Mark was concerned to show that Jesus was much more than a magician and wonderworker. Mark does this by emphasizing that Jesus wanted to see faith develop in those He helped.

The Plea of Jairus

As the synagogue ruler, Jairus may have had previous contact with Jesus. The rulers of the synagogue were responsible for the supervision of the synagogue building and arrangements for the services.

?12. How does Mark picture the growth of Jairus' faith?

The Ailing Woman

The ritual law of the Old Testament and the oral traditions of the rabbis contained many regulations governing the social situation of a woman with a discharge of blood. Such a woman was called a *zabah,* and the rules surrounding her contact with other people were considered so important that an entire chapter of the rabbinic law (*The Mishnah*) was devoted to these regulations.

❓13. Read Leviticus 15:25-27, and summarize briefly the social life this woman had led for 12 years:

It is easy to see why she made great efforts to be healed.

❓14. What steps can you see in the development of her faith in Jesus?

❓15.*Why do you think it was important that Jesus made clear that the ailing woman's *faith* was the basis of her healing and not just the fact that she touched His clothes?

Verses 35-43:

❓16. Review the situation of Jairus in verses 21-24. What are some of the emotions Jairus probably felt when the messengers arrived?

Jesus called Jairus to radical faith. When they arrived at his home the professional mourners were already there. According to rabbinic law, even the poorest man was required to hire these people to cry and wail loudly for the deceased.

Jesus used the picture of sleep to indicate death. This was

a common way of speaking about death. (Compare, for instance, 1 Thessalonians 4:13.) But He also wanted to make something else clear: He was claiming the power to wake the dead as simply as one wakes a sleeper. The crowd, though, misunderstood and thought that He was talking about normal sleep. The power of Christ over death demonstrated here is a striking promise of the ultimate victory over death at the end of the ages.

APPLYING WHAT YOU'VE LEARNED

Jesus, the Powerful Servant, concentrated on the disciples and guided them into situations in which their faith was stretched to the maximum. They were forced to think about their lives in light of His commands and to decide whether or not they were willing to let him change them.

Reflect on your own life. What are you doing right now to expose yourself to God's Word? How are you using His Word as a measuring rod for your life?

⭑ 17. What steps would you like to take to grow in each area?"

	What you are doing now	Steps you want to take
To *hear* the Word —		
To *read* the Word —		

To *study*
the Word —

To *memorize*
the Word —

 **PRINCIPLES OF GOOD
INTERPRETATION**

The Christian faith is rooted in history—the Bible is not
a book of abstract religious truths but the account of God's
invading human history to bring His creation back to Himself.

Because the Bible is an historical book which was written
with great emphasis on real events which took place in specific places with real people who spoke specific languages,
the geographical background of the Scripture is important.
It can help us understand what is being said to us through
these ancient accounts. In this study we observed the location of the incident with the demon-possessed man.

The serious Bible student should seek to gather geographical background information to the text being studied.
This is especially important for studies in the historical
accounts of the Old and New Testaments.

Good maps are often available in a Bible dictionary or
in the back of some editions of the Bible. A special Bible
atlas can also be helpful. One of the best is *The Macmillan
Bible Atlas* by Y. Aharoni and M. Avi-Yonah (New York:
Macmillan, 1968).

STUDY 9
THE FEEDING
OF THE FIVE THOUSAND

 INTRODUCTION

Jesus, the Powerful Servant, made a final teaching tour of Galilee and gave the people of that region one last opportunity to respond to His message. He sent out the Twelve on their first missionary journey through the area. This is described in Matthew 9:36-11:1, Mark 6:7-13, and Luke 9:1-6. Each of the Gospels begins at this point to focus more attention on these men—their personal reaction to Jesus, their relationship with the crowds, and the private instruction the Lord gave them. They are analyzed in a searching and honest way, and their faults are openly presented. But, they remained with Jesus! This brought them to the high point, when Peter recognized clearly that Jesus was the Messiah.

The feeding of the 5,000 plays a particularly important role in this part of the gospel story. It provides the necessary background for Christ's discussion with the disciples on the road to Jerusalem about the nature of His work as the Messiah. This miracle should have helped the Twelve recognize Jesus far earlier than they did, though. Mark makes clear that their lack of perception was due to their hardness of heart.

We will focus in this study on Mark 6:6-56. The parallel accounts are in Matthew 9-14 and in Luke 9:1-17.

 LIFE PRINCIPLE: How to handle impossible challenges.

Sometimes Jesus places us in seemingly impossible situations. True discipleship means giving Him what we have and trusting Him to provide solutions.

In this lesson:

— You will compare the parallel accounts of the mission of the Twelve in Galilee and study the impact of their activity.

— You will investigate what influence the feeding of the 5,000 had on both the disciples and the crowd, and study the background to their responses.

— You will consider how you can have a deeper fellowship with other Christians and more truly reflect God's plan for His people.

 **INVESTIGATION**

Read: Mark 6:6-56

Mark 6:6-13 — The Mission of the Twelve in Galilee

Mark and the other writers carefully prepared for their account of the sending of the Twelve on this mission. Now the point had come when Jesus directly involved them in the work He had begun. Their short mission was to be a model of their future task in the whole world. They were commissioned to be His ambassadors in *word*—by proclaiming His message—and in *power*—by doing His works.

? 1. Compare Mark 6:8,9 with the parallels in Luke 9:3 and Matthew 10:9,10. What immediate difficulties do you observe?

Sometimes, as we have seen before, we do not have enough information to "harmonize" the accounts in the Gospels with one another. This, however, is not an indication of historical unreliability. On the contrary, the basic agreement of independent witnesses strengthens the case for trustworthiness. Since the time of the early church, there have been various suggestions regarding the "staff or rod" and the sandals. In regard to the sandals, it is clear that Jesus did not expect the disciples to go barefoot! He was prohibiting the taking of extra footgear. The central point, though, is not the provisions the disciples were to take. It is the fact that they were to have absolute faith in God's provision for them. They were not to take even the smallest copper coin nor carry the traditional beggar's bag to gather their provisions. They were to leave behind the customary second tunic for keeping out the night chill in case they had to sleep in the open. God would move people to open their hearts and homes to the messengers.

Verses 10,11: When the twelve experienced warm hospitality they were not to dishonor their host by moving to more comfortable lodgings if they were offered.

If they did not receive a positive reception, they were told to "shake the dust off your feet." It was the custom of devout Jewish travelers coming from Gentile lands to shake all dust off their feet when entering the Holy Land. For the disciples to do such a thing upon leaving a Jewish village was a declaration that in God's eyes the village was pagan; it was being turned over to judgment.

❓2. According to Luke 10:16, why was rejection of the messengers filled with such drastic consequences?

Mark 6:30-34: The Return of the Twelve

Skipping over Mark's account of the death of John the Baptist, we read in these verses about the return of the disciples from their trip and the report they gave to the Lord. At that point Christ proposed a retreat for rest and recovery.

> And the people saw them going, and many recognized them, and they ran there together on foot from all the cities, and got there ahead of them! (verse 33)

Mark is clearly underlining the fact that the multitude came in response to the disciples' presence, as well as to see Jesus. Their mission was beginning to bear fruit!

Jesus "felt compassion for them [the crowd] because they were like sheep without a shepherd" (verse 34).

This saying has deep roots in the Old Testament tradition.

❓3. Read Ezekiel 34:1-6. Who were the "shepherds of

Israel" who had neglected their responsibilities and misused their position for their own gain?

? 4. See Ezekiel 34:22-24. What had God promised to do when his "flock" was misused in this way because it did not have a true Shepherd?

? 5. How was this promise fulfilled by the ministry of Jesus, the Powerful Servant? Compare also John 10:11-18.

Mark then introduces the account of the feeding of the five thousand. Through his careful preparation and from hints in the Old Testament background he was able to point clearly to the deeper meaning of the events.

Mark 6:35-46 — Bread in the Wilderness

The writers of the Gospels apparently regarded the feeding of the five thousand as crucial for understanding Jesus' identity and His work.

Jesus confronted the disciples with a problem. He seems to have deliberately created the test situation.

? 6. Read the parallel record in John 6:1-14. What do you think was Christ's purpose in creating this test situation?

The Lord made it clear that the disciples were to provide for the people. But the disciples were completely unprepared for this challenge. They reacted with a rude exaggeration. They claimed that an ordinary worker's annual wages would not buy enough for that crowd!!

? 7.*What do you think made the disciples react this way?

Verses 39,40: The crowd was organized into table groups. The arrangement recalls the order of the Israelite camp under Moses in the Old Testament.

The meal itself was a picture of the final meal that all believers in Christ will enjoy together with Him at the end of the ages. It was also a sign of the coming meal of the Lord's Supper that Jesus later instituted.

Verse 41: Jesus gives thanks.

It was the duty of every Jewish host to give thanks to God before and after the meal. The only difference from normal practice was that Jesus looked up toward heaven instead of downward.

Unlike non-biblical miracle stories from the time of the New Testament, the Gospel accounts do NOT describe the actual mechanics of the miracle itself. We do not know, for example, whether the food multiplied in Jesus' hands or in the disciples' hands.

Jesus' provision of food in the wilderness is a strong echo of parts of the Old Testament. One can see this especially in the subsequent discussion on the following day with the crowd. (John 6)

Verse 43: A small wicker basket was carried by every Jewish man as part of his outfit. It was used to hold odds and ends.

The true significance of this messianic meal was hidden from the multitude. They did not recognize who Jesus really was; instead, they tried to fit Him into their own categories. The disciples, though, were pulled into the affair by Jesus himself. He tried to help them understand the meaning of the event. However, in spite of this opportunity, they too failed to grasp the implications of the miracle.

Verses 45-46: Jesus abruptly sent the disciples away in their boat while he dismissed the crowd. This suggests a crisis atmosphere which Mark does not explain.

8. According to John 6:14,15, what was the actual background to Jesus' actions?

9.*Jesus consistently retreated for prayer when He faced conflict or temptation. What temptation was He facing in John 6:14,15?

After the night incident on the sea, the crowds gathered again the next day. They do not seem to have been receptive to Jesus' proclamation of the Word. They only wanted to see His works of power.

10.*According to John 6:15 and 25-27, what was uppermost in the minds of those who were seeking Jesus?

11. Read Acts 5:33-39 and Acts 21:37-40. What was the Jewish social and political background of the problem?

12.*What response from the people was Jesus hoping for, according to John 6:28,29?

APPLYING WHAT
YOU'VE LEARNED

There is a strong emphasis in this section of the Gospels on the close fellowship between Jesus and His disciples and on the impact they made on the people. "The people saw them going and many recognized them."

True Christianity is not a solitary religion that is to be practiced in isolation. The author of Hebrews writes: "Let us consider how to stimulate one another to love and good deeds" (Hebrews 10:24).

This reflects the need for us to be committed to a group of fellow Christians with whom we can have an open and transparent relationship.

Consider the following questions:

13. Are there other Christians with whom you have a relationship like this?

14. Do you encourage one another the way the book of Hebrews talks about?

❓15. What practical steps should you take this week to build up other believers?

PRINCIPLES OF GOOD INTERPRETATION

In this study we looked at a somewhat puzzling section in the Gospels—the description of the provisions the disciples were to take on their Galilean mission. We discovered that we do not have enough information to harmonize the accounts in the different Gospels. This illustrates an important point in regard to the interpretation of Scripture:

> Not all parts of Scripture are equally clear to our understanding.

We might wish it were otherwise, but God chose to communicate His Word in human language. Some statements in the Bible are therefore clearer than others. This does NOT mean that all statements of the Scripture are open to any interpretation one might wish to read into them. The great central teachings of the faith are clear and understandable. The Holy Spirit helps us understand and apply these truths through the help of other members in the body of Christ. However, we must learn to live with a curiosity about the unclear truths. This side of heaven, we will never have the answers to all of our questions. So we need to allow one another freedom in areas where the Scripture is not one hundred percent clear. Augustine, the great philosopher and

witness of Christ, summed up in a nutshell what our attitude
should be:

> "In the essentials, unity; in the secondary issues, freedom;
> but in all things—love!"

STUDY 10
THE TURNING POINT—
PETER'S CONFESSION
AND THE TRANSFIGURATION

 INTRODUCTION

The central issue which confronts every person who hears the story of Christ is, "Who is this Jesus?" This is the key question in every effort to communicate faith in Christ to modern people. The center of attention must not be the moral and ethical implications of Christian belief, important as these are. It must not be abstract theological theories. The spotlight must be focused on Christ. In comparison to Him, everything else is secondary.

The Gospels have two great overarching themes:

THE PERSON
JESUS

THE WORK OF
JESUS

The gospel story reaches its summit when the disciples recognize that Jesus, the Powerful Servant, is the Messiah. Each of the first three Gospels builds up to this high point. The entire first half of Mark, for instance, is characterized by intense questioning about WHO Jesus is. This is settled by Peter's great proclamation, "You are the Messiah!" Then, in the second half of his gospel, Mark turns his attention to the question, "What is the WORK Christ came to accomplish?" This is paralleled in Matthew and Luke. After the disciples had recognized who He was, Christ began to correct their confused and clouded notions of what His work was to be. Peter's great confession and the account of the transfiguration are the subject of our study. We will concentrate our attention on Mark's account in Mark 8:27-9:8.

 LIFE PRINCIPLE: How to learn from the experiences of the disciples.

To follow Jesus as His disciple means to follow Him to the cross. True discipleship does not bring worldly power and glory but death and suffering.

In this lesson:

— You will recognize why Peter's confession of Jesus as the Messiah is a dramatic turning point.

— You will compare parallel passages of Scripture to help you understand what happened at the transfiguration.

— You will review your studies on the life of Christ and meditate on how to apply them to your own life.

 INVESTIGATION

Read: Mark 8:27-9:8.

Mark 8:27-30 — Peter Recognizes the Messiah

These verses occupy the center-stage in the Gospel according to Mark and a prominent place in Matthew and

Luke (Matthew 16:13-16; Luke 9:18-20). Mark carefully developed the setting for this scene. Following his opening words, "The beginning of the Gospel about Messiah Jesus," he organized the accounts, and all of Mark 1-8 leads up to these particular verses. Everything that follows is an explanation of what Messiahship means.

Mark makes clear that the disciples were not in themselves capable of grasping the true identity of Jesus.

❓1. Compare Matthew 16:13-17. What additional light does Matthew shed on the source of Peter's sudden insight?

This was only a first step, though. Peter and the other disciples still had great misunderstandings about what Messiahship really involved. The long road to Jerusalem and the cross was about to begin. If Jesus was truly the Messiah, then what were the implications for His mission and for those who would follow Him? All three synoptic Gospels record that on the way to Jerusalem Jesus gave three major prophetic glimpses of His future suffering and death:

Mark 8:31-33 (Matthew 16:21-28; Luke 9:22-27)

Mark 9:30-32 (Matthew 17:22-23; Luke 9:43-45)

Mark 10:32-34 (Matthew 20:17-19; Luke 18:31-33)

It is crucially important to notice that immediately following each of these prophecies Jesus explained the cost and true nature of discipleship. The gospel writers wanted their readers to have a clear understanding of what being a disciple of Jesus involves. If one follows Jesus as Messiah, then one follows Him to the cross and patterns one's life after His. On the way to Jerusalem, Jesus struggled to help the disciples understand two bedrock facts:

(1) The Messiah was to be killed—this was central to His

life and work as the Son and Powerful Servant of God.

(2) To follow the Messiah does not lead to worldly glory and power but to serving others, to death and suffering.

The Gospels place these two teachings at the heart of their story.

❷2.*Why do you think the disciples had such a difficult time understanding and accepting these teachings?

Mark 8:31-9:1 — Jesus Predicts His Death

After Peter declared that Jesus was the Messiah, Jesus began to teach the Twelve what his Messiahship implied. The word "Messiah" does not appear in Jesus' explanation, though! He uses another term, "Son of Man." He links this to a dramatic prophecy, "The Son of Man must suffer . . ."

The title "Son of Man" has been a battlefield of discussion among Bible scholars. The enormous amount of literature about it is almost beyond the capacity of a single person to master. Nevertheless, it is important to try to grasp what it means and why Jesus used it.

The title probably comes from Daniel 7:13, where a glorious divine ruler is pictured as coming to rescue God's people at the end of the ages. Some see sources outside the Old Testament, but the actual evidence for these other sources existing at the time of Jesus is very weak.

Some critics insist, though, that Jesus could not possibly have used the title "Son of Man" in speaking of Himself. There is a reason for this. The real rub for these scholars comes because they realize that this implies that Jesus claimed divine authority. They argue that this would be a claim no sane man or good man would make. They are thus forced to argue against the reliability of the reports in the Gospels. But, isn't this really avoiding the issue? There is plenty of evidence in the New Testament that Christ did in fact claim to have divine authority. It is not truly honest to twist the facts to fit one's preconceptions. We are bound by honesty to squarely face the issue that the gospel writers want us to confront: Who was this person Jesus of Nazareth, who could call himself the "Son of Man"?

Why did Jesus use this title?

(1) Jesus probably used the title "Son of Man" because its exact meaning was ambiguous. This ambiguity served His purpose of concealing His identity from those who were following Him because of His wonder-working power. There is good evidence that the term could be used as a roundabout way of saying "I," much as the English expression "one" in sentences like "One hopes . . ." or "One would expect. . . ." Hostile listeners were caught off balance. They were not sure whether Jesus was identifying Himself as the divine figure from Daniel or simply referring to Himself in a roundabout way. It was not until Jesus' trial before the supreme court that they saw the real implication of the term.

(2) The title "Messiah" was too weighed down with the political hopes and dreams of the Jewish people. Jesus used the title "Son of Man" because He was not willing to be used to support the political aims of the anti-Roman faction.

(3) Jewish scholars have discovered that "no man can be defined as a Messiah before he has accomplished the task of the Anointed." A person had to do the work of the Messiah before the title could be rightfully claimed. After His resurrection Jesus did use the title "Messiah," and even discussed His Messiahship with the disciples; (Luke 24:26-28).

(4) Jesus could link the title to both His suffering and to His future glory. Suffering and glory were linked in the picture of the Son of Man from Daniel and the suffering of the godly. Christ used the title to show that He who would suffer is the same one who would one day return

in glory. The early church noted this carefully, though the believers did not use His favorite title in their daily life and worship because "Son of Man" related to Jesus' past (suffering) and future (glory). In the meantime He was their "Messiah" and "Lord."

Verses 31-33: The first prophecy of the cross

Shortly after his great confession, Peter found himself in a confrontation with the Lord. He directly contradicted Jesus' prediction of the crucifixion.

3.*Why do you think Peter reacted so strongly to Jesus' prophecy of the cross?

4.*Why do you think Jesus called Peter "Satan"? Does Christ's wording of the rebuke help us understand what He meant?

Verse 34-9:1: The requirement of following Jesus

The metaphor of taking up the cross must have been repulsive to Jesus' hearers. Death by crucifixion was a common sight in Palestine under the Romans. Jesus pictures a "death march," where the condemned man carried the cross-beam on his back to the place of his execution.

5. In verses 36-38 Jesus explains briefly what this picture implies. Summarize what He had in mind.

?6. How does Jesus describe the world-system in verse 38?

Christ made a startling claim in verse 38:

?7. What is the final criterion for a person's acceptance or rejection at the Last Judgment?

Mark 9:1—"And He was saying to them . . ." introduces a new topic. This phrase points to the fact that this is probably just the central point of a longer teaching session.

"Truly I say to you, there are some of those who are standing here who shall not taste death until they see the kingdom of God after it has come with power."

Entire systems of interpretation have been built around this single, puzzling verse. Some theologians feel Jesus was mistaken—that He expected the world to end in the lifetime of His hearers. Before we charge Jesus with such a capital error, though, it is important to look carefully at what He actually said.

?8. Jesus stated that some of the group around Him would have a unique experience. What exactly did He say:

that they would see?

in regard to when this would take place?

We must go on to the next section to see if it sheds any light on what Jesus meant.

Mark 9:2-8 — The Transfiguration

One of the key rules for interpreting a difficult scripture passage is to ask whether other passages help to explain it. Almost all the early Christians understood Jesus' prediction to refer to what happened six days later at the Transfiguration. Peter's second letter supports this interpretation.

⊘ 9. According to 2 Peter 1:16,17, what did Peter and the others see on the mountain?

The description of the transfiguration cuts straight across our modern prejudices. We ask, "How is such a thing possible?" People who have been dead for hundreds of years suddenly appear. They hold a rational discussion with Jesus while Peter, James and John look on and listen. But, perhaps our generation can accept this more readily than our grandfathers could. Since Albert Einstein launched modern physics, scientists have become uncomfortably aware that time and space are not the unbending absolutes they once seemed to be.

If the disciples were actually seeing these things take place it means that the veil of time and space parted for just a few hours and the two greatest prophets of Israel stepped through from eternity. If that were true regarding past time and space, is it so hard to accept the fact that the thin partition of time cracked open and the disciples were able to catch a glimpse of the end of history as well?

Sometimes, when walking in the mountains before sunrise, one can see the sunlight blazing on the snowy peaks long before the foothills are shaken out of darkness. In God's plan for history, two great peaks stand out as signals of the dawn that is coming when Christ returns: the transfiguration and the resurrection. They are signals for what is coming. They are signposts of the glory and power of God's kingdom. The transfiguration points to to the glory of the resurrection and the resurrection points to the coming return of the King.

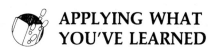 10.*How do you think Peter and the others felt about being part of the events on the mountain?

APPLYING WHAT YOU'VE LEARNED

11. What lessons do you want to apply to your own life from the experience of the disciples:

in your relationship to Christ?

in your attitudes and actions toward other people?

in your relationship to the world system and its values?

PRINCIPLES OF GOOD
INTERPRETATION

Through our study of the transfiguration we saw how important it is to compare one passage of Scripture with other passages in order to arrive at a balanced interpretation. Second Peter 1:16,17 helped us to interpret Mark 9:1 correctly. The classic Christian teaching has been that "Scripture interprets Scripture." This does not exclude the help of the Holy Spirit through other believers and Christian tradition, but it does underline the fact that the Spirit usually uses the Scripture itself (often through other Christians' teaching) to clear up our questions or to shed light on a difficult passage. The first question to ask when faced with a difficult text is, "Does any other Bible passage shed light on this?"

Editions of the Bible with "cross references" such as the *New American Standard Bible*, the *Harper Study Bible* or the *Thompson Chain Reference Bible* can provide help in finding other verses that may aid in understanding the ones studied.

LOOKING AHEAD

This study marks the half-way point of your study of the life of Christ. Now the way up to Jerusalem and the cross begins.

The undercurrent of conflict between Jesus, the Powerful Servant, and the religious and political leaders would soon erupt into open attacks on Him.

Lessons 1-10 in the second workbook (*Jesus, The Powerful Savior*) investigate the road to the cross and Christ's great lessons on discipleship. You will learn in these studies how to experience His joy in any situation. The final days in Jerusalem will come alive for you as you discover what was behind Jesus' conflict with the high priest and the details of His arrest, trials, crucifixion and resurrection.